Creative Crafts from
ROCKS & GEMSTONES

Marshall Cavendish London & New York

Edited by Isabel Moore

Published by
Marshall Cavendish Publications Limited
58 Old Compton Street
London W1V 5PA

© Marshall Cavendish Limited 1975, 1976

Parts of this material were first published
by Marshall Cavendish Limited in the partwork
Crafts

This volume first published 1976

Printed in Great Britain by
Severn Valley Press, Caerphilly

ISBN 0 85685 175 2

Introduction

Rocks and gemstones have fascinated Man almost since the beginning of time, and the passage of years shows no signs of lessening the attraction. 'Rock hounding' and the fashioning of beautiful things from rocks and gemstones are, in fact, two of the fastest growing hobbies in the country.

Creative Crafts from Rocks and Gemstones is therefore a timely book, specially produced as a practical, comprehensive guide to all who would like to participate in both the fascination and the hobby. It follows the history of stones, discusses how to find and recognize them, then how to create from them finished, smooth stones by tumbling and polishing, and by the more advanced techniques of cutting them into cabochons and facets.

The heart of the book is devoted to a whole section of ideas on what to do with your finished stones—from pretty, individualized jewellery made with findings or by the wire-wrapping method (with explicit and simple step by step instructions and lots of lavish illustrations of the stunning finished products), to useful and decorative objects, such as mirrors, bookends, room dividers, table tops—all transformed from prosaic usefulness into items of aesthetic, unique appeal.

Anyone who has ever been moved by the beauty of a rock or stone will find here all they need to turn this interest into an absorbing and creative pastime.

Contents

The History of Rocks & Gemstones

Ancient man first used rocks and stones for purely practical purposes —to make tools such as hammers, scrapers, axes and spear points.

Flint was the most popular material used by these early men but there is evidence that quartz, chalcedony, chert, jasper and obsidian were also utilized. With the appearance of Cro-Magnon man (some 25,000 years ago), there were improvements in tool-making and stone-working, and for the first time there is evidence of stone, shell and animal teeth being used for non-utilitarian articles, such as necklaces and other items of personal adornment.

By 3500 BC great civilizations had developed independently in Mesopotamia (the land between the Tigris and Euphrates, roughly modern-day Syria), in China along the Yangtze River, in India along the Indus and in Egypt along the Nile. All of these early cultures cultivated crops, invented forms of writing, built cities, worked in stones and metals, and attained great skill in the lapidary arts. The Sumerians, who developed the first great culture in Mesopotamia, were skilled carvers of stones and metals. Excavations at Ur of the Chaldees have unearthed many beautiful examples of their work—delicate statues, intricate mosaics of shell and lapis lazuli, cylinders of semi-precious stones, and jewellery.

Carved gemstones came first from China, where beautiful ornaments and jewellery were made, particularly of jade. Jade, in fact, was regarded almost in mystical terms in ancient China, believed to be a product of Heaven itself and, as such, endowed with special magical healing powers. In India, too, were made intricate carvings and jewellery from jade, particularly by the Moguls, and it is here that the art of cutting and polishing stones seems to have been developed. Body adornment, generally, was so popular in India, in fact, that, rather than adapt clothing to changes in climate, fashionable early Indians merely decked themselves in ever heavier jewellery!

The lapidary arts of these ancient cultures travelled along the caravan trade routes, from China to Mesopotamia, from India to Egypt and to and from Greece and Rome. The trade seems to have been extensive; jade from China has been found in Assyrian ruins while turquoise from

Above *Two scarabs from Ancient Egypt.*

Far Left *A selection of cut and polished gemstones.*

Near Left *Carnelian and steatite beads worn by women from the ancient Indus civilizations.*

5

Egypt has been discovered in India. Without question the crafts of stone-working and jewellery-making reached their peak in ancient Egypt, where they were woven into the fabric of everyday life and religion.

Stone-work ranged from the carving of tiny, exquisite amulets of semi-precious stones, often in the shape of the sacred scarab beetle, to mighty monuments such as the Sphinx and the Great Pyramid of Gizeh.

The religion of ancient Egypt was based on a strong belief in life after death, and much effort and time went into building temples to the gods, burial places for the kings, and into preparing the thousands of items needed by the royal dead to use on their journey to the other world. The discovery, in the Valley of Kings near Thebes, of the tomb of the boy-king Tutankhamen, has provided archaeologists with a rich haul of artifacts from the time of the Pharaohs. It was a positive treasure trove of bowls of gold, alabaster vases and lamps, ivory chests and a Pharaoh's throne, carved with elaborate likenesses of the young king and his queen, covered with gold and silver, and inlaid with semi-precious stones and coloured glass. The tomb also yielded countless items of jewellery—strings of beads, of carnelian and turquoise, earrings, bead collars, gold rings, armlets, chains, pectorals, even a gilt chest filled with jewels and amulets. And finest of all was the burial chamber itself: a sarcophagus cut from yellow quartzite, with the figures of four different goddesses sculptured in bas-relief on each corner and fitted with a granite cover. Inside were three mummiform coffins; the outer an effigy of the king, in gold with inlaid eyes of obsidian and eyelids of lapis lazuli; the second also a portrait of the king covered with thick gold foil and inlaid with bright opaque glass; the third, which weighed over a ton, solid gold set with semi-precious stones. Inside was the actual mummy of the king, a gold mask covering his head and shoulders and his body richly covered with jewels of all kinds.

Although early Greek jewellery shows a predominantly Egyptian influence, later craftsmen undoubtedly developed the craft independently, taking it to new heights of achievement. It was the Greeks, for example, who were generally credited with the development of intaglio (gems with engraving sunk into them) and, in a world where even kings were often illiterate, intaglio rings and ornaments had an important and necessary use as a seal, or signature, on important documents. The Greeks also invented the converse of intaglio, cameo (gems with engraving raised in relief on the surface). Cameos seem to have been basically decorative rather than useful right from the start, and often were portraits of sovereigns, religious or mythological figures.

By the end of the Roman empire, crafting in rocks and gemstones had declined drastically; no new developments had occurred and examples of jewellery and ornaments found in excavations suggest that a dramatic decline in the quality of workmanship and skill also took place.

And there the craft rested until the Middle Ages, with most gemstones still being either cut with tools, which ranged from extremely to fairly primitive, or, in the case of harder stones, by drilling with a wheel, a method still known as cabochon, which consists of 'rounding off' or shaping the edges of the stones and slicing them flat on the underside. However, in the late 1600's the technique of faceting was developed, which revolutionized the use of transparent gems. Faceting was probably developed in Holland and although it was—and is—a somewhat wasteful method of cutting stones (only half of the original remains after cutting), it increases their value by keeping only the purest part, and also the brilliance and appearance of the gem. Thus the appearance-conscious rich of the late Middle Ages could display their collection of diamonds, emeralds and sapphires, to even greater advantage!

And since life in general, and the life of the rich and noble in particular, became more and more stylized and ostentatious during this time, this display was not limited to the wearing of elaborate jewellery alone—precious and semi-precious stones were often actually sewn into many items of apparel.

Ornaments, too, became more than merely decorative, and often taste

One of the most exciting archaeological finds of the century occurred when Howard Carter discovered the tomb of the boy-king Tutankhamen. The mask of the Pharaoh, right, is one of the most beautiful of the many artifacts found in the tomb.

The art of working in rocks and gemstones reached new heights of ostentation and skill in Imperial Russia. The great jeweller Fabergé fashioned the three pieces illustrated on the right; the centre piece is the now famous jewelled Easter egg, a gift from the Czar to his wife.

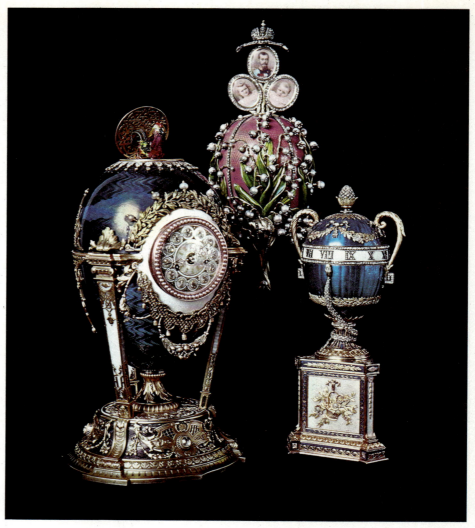

and common sense were lost in the general scramble to cram as many priceless gems as possible on to one small surface. Occasionally, however, opulence was combined with exquisite taste and workmanship and perhaps this form of ostentatious crafting of rocks and gemstones reached its peak in nineteenth century Czarist Russia, where a jeweller of French descent called Peter Karl Fabergé, fashioned ornaments and jewellery for the royal household. His most famous creations were the elaborately jewelled Easter eggs, first commissioned by Czar Alexander III for his wife. The eggs attained a splendour rarely matched even in that opulent court, and displayed an exquisiteness of touch which makes them still truly unique works of art.

In the early Americas

Ancient man first came to the Americas about 40,000 years ago. As the number of migrants increased, they moved southwards and fanned out, moving down into the area that is now Mexico, then further southwards into Central and South America. Here, in the total isolation made possible by two oceans, there evolved completely unique cultures, arts, religions, and mighty empires. A dozen or more civilizations developed, flowered, then declined or were destroyed by invaders from other tribes or alien cultures.

Jade, gold and silver were all found in great abundance in Central and South America and were, therefore, the materials most often used to make ornaments and jewellery. The Olmecs, the first of the great cultures to flourish, who lived in an area roughly equivalent to the modern lowlands of the Gulf of Mexico, considered jade to be the most precious of all stones—as did the later Mayans, Zapotecs and Aztecs. They carved (with tools that were primitive in the extreme—no culture in the early Americas achieved an Iron Age) delicate

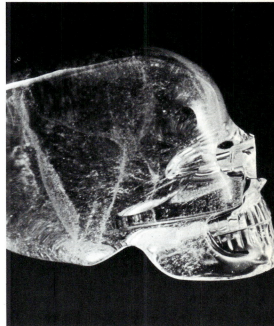

Left *A dagger of gold inlaid with turquoise from the Chimus of South America. They were eventually conquered and their ideas incorporated into the great Inca civilization.*
Above *An Aztec skull fashioned in crystal.*

statues and intricate figurines, masks, pendants and effigies.

Culture reached its peak in Meso-America with the advent of the Maya whose civilization spans about 600 years from 300 to 900 AD. In their great ceremonial cities (with exotic names like Tikal and Chichen-Itza) their lapidaries produced a great variety of jewellery—mostly in the inevitable jade, gold and silver—but crafted to new heights of intricacy and beauty.

There is some circumstantial evidence to suggest that, like the Chinese, the Mayans believed that jade had life-giving, or at least preserving, qualities; the sarcophagus of an ancient Mayan priest or chieftain unearthed at Palenque contained a mosaic jade death mask made from over 200 pieces of jade, as well as rings, necklaces and ear plugs.

The Aztecs were basically warriors but, like all successful warrior tribes, they incorporated the best of the civilizations they conquered into their own. As a result, although they did not themselves perhaps produce much that was unique in cultural terms, they adapted, improved and developed the best of what their conquered tribes had to offer. Their capital of Tenochtitlan (on the site of present-day Mexico City) was the largest city in the world at the time of Cortes' arrival in 1519—over 300,000 people dwelt there in approximately 60,000 houses —and contained the finest artisans, many from the culturally advanced Mixtec tribe, capable of producing items of exquisite beauty from jade, turquoise, rock crystal, emeralds, pearls, silver and gold. A special emerald green jade, named by the Aztecs *quetzalchalchihuitl* after the brilliant plumage of the quetzal bird, was particularly prized.

The Inca was the last and, arguably, the greatest of the early American civilizations. The Incas, like the Romans and Aztecs, were great adapters of other people's talents— in their case the arts and sculptures of the Chimú. It was in the crafting of silver and, particularly, gold, that the Inca civilization excelled. (Gold was hammered, then embossed and used as wall coverings for the great palaces and temples—the great Temple of the Sun in the Inca capital Cuzco, for instance, literally had walls of gold.) But they also encouraged their artisans to fashion jewellery in rocks and gemstones, including bracelets, rings, ear plugs, pendants and special mirrors of jet, which were used to foretell the future.

In myth and medicine
From the very earliest times, many gemstones had attributed to them special and quite specific powers, most of a semi-mystic or even medicinal nature so that those who wore amulets or bracelets containing the stones were considered to be 'protected' against evil spells and enchantments. Turquoise, for instance, was popularly supposed to ward off danger, while diamonds were believed to endow their wearer with strength in battle; the carbuncle had an even greater task to perform—to make its wearer disappear!

As an adjunct to this, perhaps, different gemstones were gradually assigned to each month of the year, for instance opal, amethyst and amber were assigned to the astrological sign of Aquarius (January 20–February 18), and the belief held that should people born in that month wear 'their' stone, they would

Below Left *An ancient pi disc carved in jade. The disc occupied roughly the same place in ancient Chinese religious life as does the Cross in modern Christianity.*
Below Right *An Aztec dagger made of chalcedony. The Aztecs used these daggers to tear the hearts from living human sacrifices to appease their gods.*
Right *A jade funerary mask from the ancient Mexican city of Tenochtitlan the site of present-day Mexico City.*

be endowed with supernatural protection and granted prosperity and good fortune.

Man has always been anxious to know what fate has in store for him, and rocks and gemstones have played their part in divination, too: that crystal ball, still popular with fortune tellers today, was known in ancient Greece, among the Assyrians and in early India, and in those days was probably a genuine piece of rock crystal. Crystallomancy, or scrying as it is sometimes called, was in fact revered in early times, and it was considered a dignified profession to engage in as late as the Middle Ages, when Queen Elizabeth I of England had an official court astrologer who practised crystallomancy.

It was probably only a short step from feeling 'protected' by certain stones, and relying on them to predict the future, to attributing to them special curative powers. This was particularly prevalent among primitive cultures but by no means confined to them; as late as the Middle Ages, Pope Clement VII is reported to have been given medicine of pulverized gemstones. Most of the cultures of South America believed that jade prevented diseases of the kidney and groin—a belief carried back to Europe by the Spanish *conquistadors*, where it became a firmly entrenched piece of folklore. And several other gemstones had their powers, too—sapphires, to take one instance, were popularly supposed to prevent diseases of the eye.

In religion

The association of rocks and gemstones with religion, and their incorporation into the religious fabric of society, came early in time and seems to span most of the world's major religions; it was, in fact at bottom, simply an extension of the semi-medicinal, mystic powers attributed to certain stones. Jade was incorporated into Chinese religion from the beginning; it was used in religious ceremonies, and the ancient solar disk of jade occupied roughly the same place in religious life in early China as does the Cross in modern Christianity. In China, and to a lesser extent in Arabia, Persia

and parts of India, jade was also placed in the mouth of the newly dead because it was believed to have life-giving properties.

By Old Testament times, stones were firmly incorporated into the religious ritual of the tribes of Israel, and often appeared on priestly garments. In Exodus, for example, the Lord instructs Moses as to how the holy garments of the high priest (his brother Aaron) are to be prepared: ' . . . And they shall make an ephod of gold, of purple and scarlet stuff, and of fine twisted linen, skilfully worked. It shall have two shoulder-pieces attached to its two edges, that it may be joined together . . . And you shall take two onyx stones and engrave on them the names of the sons of Israel, six of their names on one stone and the names of the remaining six on the other stone, in the order of their birth. As a jeweller engraves signets, so shall you engrave the two stones . . . you shall enclose them in settings of gold filigree. And you shall set the two stones upon the shoulder-pieces of the ephod . . . and you shall attach the corded chains

to the settings. And you shall make a breastplate of judgment, in skilled work—like the world of the ephod you shall make it, of gold, blue and purple and scarlet stuff, and fine twisted linen . . . And you shall set in it four rows of stones. A row of sardius, topaz and carbuncle shall be the first row; and the second row an emerald, a sapphire and a diamond; and the third row a jacinth, an agate and an amethyst; and the fourth row a beryl, an onyx and a jasper; they shall be set in gold filigree. There shall be 12 stones with their names according to the names of the sons of Israel; they shall be like signets, each engraved with its name, for the 12 tribes.'

The Aztec religion was based on worship of the sun. A great deal of their ritual took the form of appeasing and 'nourishing' the sun so that it would not fall from the heavens— and this 'nourishment' took the form of human sacrifice, usually of young girls who were despatched to the sun by an ornate ritual dagger made of chalcedony. The ceremony was an elaborate one, presided over by the war-god Huichilobos, who is

The priestly robes described in Exodus are rich and ornate – and set with various precious and semi-precious jewels. The pectoral was one of the most elaborate, being worn over the ephod, set with 12 stones, each one representing one of the tribes of Israel and inscribed with its name.

The identification of the stones is difficult, although a list is given in the Bible. They were set in gold on a breastplate eight or nine inches square and since they were engraved (with the appropriate tribe's name), they were probably quite large. The engraving also suggests that the stones were soft, as ancient tools would have made little impression on hard surfaces.

The stones shown in the above picture have all been suggested as possible types by Biblical scholars. All are reasonably common and have been shown by archaeologists to have been used for decoration in ancient times.

From left to right they are: carnelian, amazonite, jasper, amber, agate, amethyst, turquoise, lapis lazuli, chalcedony, mother of pearl, black onyx and jasper onyx.

described as being 'girdled with huge snakes made of gold and precious stones . . . Around his neck hung some Indian faces and other objects in the shape of hearts, the former made of gold and the latter of silver, with many precious blue stones.'

In early Australia, too, rocks and gemstones played their part in religion. Many of the southern Aboriginal tribes worshipped the rock crystal, and although they do not seem to have ascribed to it any powers of divination, they did believe it to possess supernatural qualities which helped the human spirit transform itself beyond space and time.

As symbols of authority

In earliest times, plebians were actually forbidden to wear jewellery, and adornment thus became a badge of rank, then of authority. By Greek times, the crown or coronet, in those days a simple circlet of gold with one stone set in it, had become the symbol of ultimate authority, the king. Through the centuries, as other costumes became more richly adorned and flamboyant, so did the crown, which gradually became more complex in both shape and content, culminating in the splendid affairs fashioned mostly in the Middle Ages which are still used at

European coronations. And once the simple circlet was abandoned by the monarchy, it therefore became a suitable adornment for the castes immediately below the royal—hence the ducal and baronial coronet.

Jewellery as insignia of rank was not confined to the monarchies of Europe, nor to the wearing of a crown. The Maoris of New Zealand venerated jade almost as much as did the ancient Chinese, and used it to carve the *hei-tiki*. The chieftains of the tribes wore the *hei-tiki*, a pendant of a rather squat, embryonic figure, to ensure the protection of the ancient god-king *tiki*, and as a symbol of their authority.

And as with temporal authority, so with religious. Priests of religion, in addition to their heavenly functions, traditionally were also symbols of temporal, even political authority and were, therefore, entitled to wear the jewelled insignia that their standing in the community entitled them to. Rocks and gemstones were incorporated into the ritual of religion early, and it was probably, therefore, only a short step to also using them as a symbol of churchly rank. The Episcopal ring of the Roman Catholic Church, for instance, is still worn by the upper echelons of the clergy as a symbol of their authority and the laity of the Church still show their veneration of this authority by kissing it. The Episcopal ring, today, also symbolizes something else. For although the clergy are authorized to wear rings inset with any stone or stones (except sapphire which is reserved for cardinals), an increasing number now opt for simple circlets, without stones of any description—and are thus part of a growing trend away from the ostentation of the Fabergé school of gemcrafting, back towards the simpler origins of the craft.

And since, in the beginning, most people fashioned their own ornaments and jewellery, this perhaps explains at least in part, the current revival of interest in making objects from rocks and gemstones at home. The chapters that follow amply illustrate the great satisfaction to be gained from finding, collecting and creating beautiful things in rocks and stone—whether they be for religious, mystical or merely decorative purposes.

Far Left *The crown as a symbol of regal authority: this crown was made for Queen Elizabeth the Queen Mother for her coronation in 1937. The diamond at the front of the crown is the Indian diamond known as Koh-i-Noor.*
Left *A jade Maori hei-tiki. The hei-tikis were worn by Maori chieftains to symbolize their authority and assure the protection of their ancestors.*

Finding & Collecting

The ideal hobby for most people is one that mixes the fresh air and sunshine of the great outdoors with the lure of a treasure hunt and the discovery of some of nature's most beautiful creations. 'Rockhounding' combines all these qualities with a pastime that can be practical in groups of one or one hundred. Participants in one of the fastest-growing hobbies in the English-speaking world, 'rockhounds' are people who collect rocks for the joy of it, and then by tumbling,

cutting and polishing, turn their stones into a variety of exotic treasures.

Why collect rocks?

The answers to this question are as varied as the people who ask it. As chapter 1 demonstrates, man has exhibited a fascination for rocks and gemstones, almost since the dawn of human existence. The tangible beauty of the stones themselves draws many enthusiasts to the search for gemstones: as decorative items rocks have few equals in their variety and splendour and their use in jewellery making is limitless. The rockhound hobby is both fascinating and educational. It offers outdoor adventure for the entire family, on short weekend or long vacations, or even day trips—a short Sunday walk down any country lane will yield lovely finds. And, the collecting of the stones is only the beginning phase of rockhounding. There are numerous branches of the gemcraft hobby.

Gem cutting includes the finishing of not only gemstones but of semiprecious rocks as well. There are a number of divisions of the cutting activity.

Searching for rocks and gemstones is a healthy hobby that can involve the whole family—even the smaller members, as here, can make exciting finds and learn a little geology as well!

17

Tumbling is the most popular of the gem finishing techniques and the one that most beginners take up first. It consists of placing stones, water and a grinding grit in a tumbling barrel and letting the mixture run through a series of grinding operations and one pre-polish and one polish stage. The beauty of the finished product is rewarding and serves to add impetus to the beginner's enthusiasm. This method of finishing stones is discussed at length in the next chapter.

Faceting is the cutting of flat planes on a gemstone. This is a stage usually taken up by the

advanced hobbyist.

Cabochon making consists of slicing the rock into thin slabs, trimming a portion of one of these slabs into a 'pre-form' and, then, by shaping on a grinding wheel and polishing on a buff, forming a stone (usually oval or round in shape) that is widely used in many forms of jewellery. Faceting and cabochon making are discussed in more detail in a later chapter.

Other more specialized divisions of the finishing stage include **sphere making** (the forming of a round ball from a piece of solid rock), **lapping** (the grinding and polishing of flat rock surfaces for use as bookends, paperweights, etc.) and **gemstone carving** (the carving of animals, flowers, etc. from agate, jasper or other suitable stone material).

Jewellery making consists of all forms of converting your rocks into jewellery or decorative objects. Jewellery making is also discussed in a later chapter.

Mineral collecting has a number of divisions, including the gathering of crystals, the naturally symmetrical forms that some minerals take, fluorescent minerals which glow in brilliant colours under ultraviolet light and micromounts, miniature mineral specimens so tiny that they have to be examined under magnifying glasses or low-power microscopes.

Fossil collecting is similar to mineral collecting but concentrates entirely on the remains of plant and animal life found in rock formations.

Collecting

The first step in rock collecting is to decide where and what you want to hunt. Since it is an ideal family activity, let everyone join in the planning and preparation. The entire family can participate in the rock hobby. Grandad can be just as enthusiastic as the 'pebble-pup', the name given to rockhound children. Most beginners collect anything that is beautiful or unusual or appealing. But many hobbyists go further and specialize in a single field such as collecting only mineral crystals or petrified woods or agates. Some gather only fossils.

It can be as inexpensive a hobby as you wish. Simple, found-at-home tools or a cheap, even do-it-yourself, tumbler can be used in the beginning stages. As you become more involved in the hobby, you can purchase elaborate equipment for tumbling, polishing, cutting and grinding. The choice is up to you.

Similarly, collecting can be an afternoon outing to the beach or a weekend in the desert. Or, it can be a collecting trip to a foreign land. Australia and South Africa both offer rockhound package tours to foreigners who wish to search in those countries. And combination study and collecting holidays are available to such places as Brazil, Mexico, India and the Far East.

A great deal of prior knowledge can, and should, be obtained before ever going into the field. It is very important to know what can be easily found in the area in which you have chosen to look. Or, if you have a yen to collect specific kinds of stones, you must find out the locations where they might be found. First, visit a museum with a good gem and mineral collection to become familiar with the actual stones, what they look like in their

Below Far Left *Sawing Purbeck stone at St. Aldhems Quarry. A cross-cut saw is being used, with water to cool the blade, mixed with abrasive to cut the stone.*

Above Left *Members of a gem club search for stones near Beechworth, an old gold-mining area in Victoria, Australia.*

Below Left *Mining Carrara marble in Italy. Large pieces are separated first, then cut into smaller pieces on the site. Michelangelo is said to have used Carrara marble from this same quarry.*

A beautiful piece of clear quartz in Dolamite, found in its natural state.

natural and polished states, and what can be done with them. Another excellent source of information is to visit a 'rock show' near your home. Thousands are held each year around the world, where you can see an enormous variety of amateur exhibits and dealer displays. From these two sources you will be able to examine at close range most of the materials that are available. This visual knowledge of both the rough and finished rocks will serve you in later searches and guide you in what use you can make of the stones you find yourself.

Of course, numerous books and other publications are available for study. There are periodicals specializing in lapidary subjects available through local libraries and in most hobby and rock shops. And many very good books are available as well. If you like, join a rock club. Countless amateur societies exist throughout the world—a thousand or more in the USA and dozens in Great Britain, Canada, Australia, New Zealand and South Africa. Clubs have regular meetings and frequent field trips on which the members who wish to can go to a gem location and hunt together. Longtime members of these organizations are very helpful to newcomers, both at meetings and in the field. And dedicated rockhounds are a friendly breed who welcome new members very warmly.

One of the most colourful of the rock clubs is The Rollin' Rock Club. The membership numbers several thousand, and although most of the members reside in the United States, there are members from nearby Canada and from as far away as South Africa, Great Britain, Australia and New Zealand. The full name of the club is Rollin' Rock Club of Texas and Any Other State or Country of the World and Outer

Space, and the club motto is 'A rollin' stone gathers no moss, but does gain a certain polish.'

A club may have a dozen or several hundred members. And most local clubs are in turn affiliated with regional federations. Many of these federations have an annual gem and mineral exhibition in which the member clubs and individual members participate. Displays of gemstones and related lapidary arts are presented in both competitive and non-competitive classes. Most gem and mineral clubs also have annual shows of their own which are not part of a federation show. These smaller and more local shows are scattered around the world every week-end of the year. They will be listed under a 'Calendar of Events' in the magazines devoted to the lapidary hobby. By checking this calendar you can find as many as a hundred shows in an average month in some parts of the world.

Go to any of the many places where people pursue the rock hobby—seashore, mountains, river banks, deserts, mine tips, excavations and quarries, ghost towns. You will see people searching for stones—perhaps only one or two in more remote spots, but dozens in more popular areas. All are seeking, and finding, treasures to carry home

Above Far Left *Tourmaline*
Above Left *Topaz in its natural state.*
Below Far Left *Turquoise in its natural state, finely veined and marbled with various minerals.*
Below Left *A cut and polished turquoise.*

The Grand Canyon in Arizona is a breathtakingly beautiful collection of almost every type of rock.
Right *St. Covan's Rock in Wales—natural igneous rock in a natural setting.*

and fashion into a dazzling variety of ornaments and jewellery.

Basic geology

A general knowledge of basic geology will be of great help to the budding rockhound. Geology is the study of the origin, history and composition of the earth. The earth began when primordial gases and matter came together to form our planet billions of years ago, and continues as volcanic flows form new land masses. At the same time, forces such as wind, water and ice constantly erode these masses. The entire surface of the earth is covered by a relatively thin layer of rock—twenty-five to thirty miles in thickness at its maximum—which forms the earth's crust. Water covers nearly three-fourths of the

earth's surface, and the surface features of the rock beneath the oceans are similar to the land features—deep canyons, high mountains, plateaux and valleys. The thin outer crust, which is known as the 'rock mantle', consists of rock, sand and soil and is formed by the breaking up of bedrock, the solid layer of rock beneath the mantle rock.

Below the bedrock is a layer of heavier rock about 1800 miles thick known as the intermediate zone. This area consists of hot dense rocks under great pressure and is the source of volcanic activity.

Beneath this layer is the core, which extends 2000 miles to the very centre of the earth. The upper half of this core is a hot, dense liquid estimated to be nearly $3300°C(6000°F)$ and

under tremendous pressure. The lower half of the core at the centre of the world is believed to be solid and composed of nickel and iron.

The rocks that form the earth's crust are made up of different elements and minerals. An element is a substance made up of a single kind of atom. There are about ninety naturally occurring elements which, singly or in combination, compose all known substances. Eight of these ninety elements make up nearly 98 percent of the earth's crust, and two of these, oxygen and silicon, comprise three-quarters of the earth's crust.

A mineral is an inorganic substance. Some, such as diamonds, which are composed entirely of carbon, consist of one single element. But most are chemical compounds. More than 2000 minerals exist in nature, yet only a dozen of these make up 90 percent of all rocks in existence. Some minerals (principally quartz, calcite and the feldspars) appear so frequently in rocks that they are known as rock-forming minerals. Other minerals in this group include gypsum, mica

Stalactites and stalagmites are formed from carboniferous rocks—a prime example of the sedimentary type.

and hornblende. Most of the rock-forming minerals are silicates, a combination of silicon, oxygen and a specific metal.

All rocks are classified into three broad groups according to their origin and method of formation: igneous, sedimentary and metamorphic. Igneous rocks form from the cooling of molten lava known as magma, the hot liquid rock matter located deep within the earth, and are further divided into two groups based on how and where the magmas cooled.

Extrusive igneous rocks form when molten lava is erupted out of volcanic craters or fissures in the earth's crust on to the surface and cool there fairly rapidly. These contain either small crystals or show no crystallization at all. Examples of extrusive igneous rocks are basalt, pumice and rhyolite.

Intrusive igneous rocks form when the molten minerals cool and harden beneath the surface of the earth. This magma, being deeply buried, cools very slowly and the resulting intrusive rock contains large mineral crystals. Examples of intrusive igneous rocks are granite, gabbro and porphyry.

Sedimentary rocks form from particles of pre-existing rocks. Fragments are carried away by wind or running water and deposited in shallow lakes or seas, where sediments of sand, clay and silt are laid down in layers, or strata, that harden and are compressed or cemented together to form sedimentary rocks. Shells and the fossil remains of ancient plant and animal life accumulated on the bottom of the ocean and formed some sedimentary rocks. Examples of the more common sedimentary rocks are sandstone, conglomerates, shale and limestone.

Metamorphic rocks can be either sedimentary or igneous rocks, but as the name implies, they have changed form. The metamorphism is caused by the heat and extreme pressures that occur below the surface of the earth or by chemical action. These changes occur during movements of the earth's crust or when hot igneous magmas intrude into or between other rocks or rock layers. This intrusion into or between igneous or sedimentary rocks or even other metamorphic ones, produces extreme changes in the original rock, which is then metamorphosed into an entirely new material. This new form is harder, denser and more crystalline than the original rock.

By this method sandstone is changed into quartzite; limestone into marble; shale into slate; and granite into gneiss.

Recognition

Learn to recognize different kinds of rocks. Visual recognition is not something that can be learned from books. The best way to become acquainted with stones is to spend time viewing and studying mineral and rock specimens in museums or at the exhibits and displays at gem and mineral shows. Some club programmes utilize actual specimens which can be handled, examined very closely and discussed in detail. The most valuable visual knowledge will be gained.

Stones which are most popular with the amateur rockhound belong to the quartz family. Of these, agates (which come in hundreds of varieties) are the most sought-after gemstone material, and petrified woods are probably second.

Quartz is the most common of all minerals, and the quartz family contains a greater variety of gemstones than any other. Quartz occurs in two forms: crystalline (quartz crystal and smoky quartz) and cryptocrystalline (agate, flint, chert, jasper, carnelian and chalcedony). It is from this second form that most of your rock finds will come. Quartz is silicon dioxide (SiO_2) and exists in liquid form throughout the earth's surface. The many colourful rock materials in this family form in this way: silicia-laden solutions in underground waters may impregnate buried organic matter and fill cavities in extrusive igneous rocks such as basalt or rhyolite. As these mineral-bearing waters move through the earth they deposit their content within the cells of the organic matter, forming petrified wood, or fill the hollows of the volcanic crust, making the agates. Variations in colour in various stones, even of the same kind, is caused by varying amounts of mineral impurities found in the formative waters. The presence of iron in the solution will colour the rocks red, yellow or brown; dark green comes from chromium; bright apple green from nickel oxide.

Testing on the spot

Look for stones of suitable hardness, checking closely for fractures or bad chips. Discard these in the beginning, along with soft, porous or easily broken stones, such as sandstone, slate or shale.

Mention of the Mohs scale should be made here. This is an arbitrary hardness index devised by a German mineralogist over a hundred years ago and still in wide use today. The identifying list consists of ten minerals, from the softest—1, Talc, to the hardest—10, Diamond.

1. Talc
2. Gypsum
3. Calcite
4. Fluorite
5. Apatite
6. Othoclase
7. Quartz
8. Topaz
9. Corundum
10. Diamond

Any mineral on this scale can scratch any other mineral with a lower number, and can in turn be scratched by any mineral with a higher number. A set of hardness testing points tipped with actual minerals can be purchased and is useful to determine whether a rock is suitable to cut and polish.

Softer stones do not polish well nor do they wear well when used to make jewellery. In the absence of a set of hardness points, some handy items may be used in the field to ascertain approximate hardness: a fingernail has a hardness of 2; a copper coin, 3; a piece of window glass, 5; a knife blade, 6; and a metal file, 8.

Field trips

One of the greatest benefits to come from membership in a gem and mineral club is the knowledge gained from lectures and demonstrations at club meetings and from actual on-the-spot participation in the club's field trips. Some clubs have field trips quarterly; some on an every-second-month basis. A few of the more active clubs that are located in areas where severe winters are no problem may have field trips every month.

One typical American club in the course of a year visited:

1. A gravel bar on a river to collect agates, chert, corals, fossils and petrified wood.
2. A petrified forest area.
3. Sedimentary deposits to collect cretaceous fossils, quartz and petrified wood.
4. A gravel-washing plant to hunt agates, jasper and petrified wood.
5. The banks and bed of a creek to collect pyrite and fossils.
6. An open-pit mine to hunt quartz crystal clusters.

Field trip activities, which can be very helpful to the beginner, will vary with the club locality and interest. They might include, for instance, digging for fossil fish and petrified wood in Wyoming or searching for jade in British Columbia, diamonds in South Africa, jet in Yorkshire or turquoise in Nevada. It could include panning for gold in Alaska or fossicking for sapphires in Fraser's Creek or agates in Agate Creek in Australia or hunting smoky quartz in Scotland. Go where the field trips take you. It will be very rewarding in both knowledge and treasures.

Equipment

Rock hunting requires a minimum of equipment, but certain standard hiking or backpacking comfort items should be assembled. Almost everyone already uses some of these, particularly those who spend any time outdoors. First on the list should be proper footwear—sturdy shoes or boots for mountains, deserts or rough terrain; sneakers or plimsolls or waders for the beach or river banks. Include a water bottle, a knife, a hat, sturdy work gloves, sunglasses, etc.

Purely rockhound equipment needed will include:

Rock hammer These are hammers designed for geologists' use and are available in three types and several weights. The most widely used is the 'rock pick', which has a flat head on one side and a pointed pick on the other. Another design has a flat head on the front and a chisel end on the back. The third type is the chipping hammer, with a sharp, tapered head on the front and a pointed tip on the back.

Crack hammer These are small short-handled sledge hammers used, as the name implies, to crack rock or drive chisels or pry bars into a difficult rock face.

Rock Chisels Two are needed—a narrow one for working in pockets or other small areas and a large chisel for splitting and prying.

Prybar or jimmy For prying and wedging in cracks and crevices.

Shovel This should be short-handled and round-tipped. Or use a folding army-style shovel.

Safety goggles Lightweight unbreakable glass or plastic goggles to protect the eyes from flying particles when chipping pieces from a larger rock.

Round out your equipment with such items as a canvas knapsack or plastic bucket to hold your stones; 10X magnifying lens; old newspapers in which to wrap specimens; small notebook and pencil; maps of the area; compass; first aid kit, etc.

Dangers

A word of warning about the hazards involved. Caution and common sense should be all that are needed. Keep general safety precautions in mind. Do not go alone into isolated areas or in rough terrain. Travel with at least one other companion in unknown territory. Be sure to have plenty of water and food along. Vehicles should be in good repair; always have adequate extra petrol and spare tyres along.

At the seashore be extremely cautious of tricky tides and never be caught in places without easy egress during rising tides.

Watch for falling rocks from cliffs and overhangs. Never work directly above or below another rockhound. In certain regions, snakes are a menace and precautions should be taken. In such areas it is wise to have along a snake-bite kit as well as a first-aid kit, which should always be carried into the field as basic equipment.

Other dangers include treacherous ground, quicksand, rock slides, pits hidden by undergrowth or water-filled excavations and cave-ins. Beware of old, abandoned mine tunnels; these are usually filled with rotten timbers and ladders, flooded shafts and, hardest to detect but most dangerous of all, pockets of poisonous gases.

Simple courtesy should always be observed. Obtain permission to hunt in gravel pits or quarries—or anywhere on private property. Leave gates as you find them. Put out all fires. Do not leave garbage or other debris behind.

Equipment is essential if you wish to become a serious rock hound, and perhaps the most essential single piece of equipment is the rock hammer or pick.

Amazonite

Pink Botswana

Bowenite

Lace Agate

Fancy Bloodstone

Blue Lace Agate

Aventurine

Amethyst

Rutilated Quartz

Rock Crystal

Moroccan Beans

Tumbling & Polishing

Tumbling is the process that smooths and polishes pebbles and stones so that they are ready for use as jewellery or any other decoration. It is done with a tumbling machine, which runs from an ordinary power point in the home. This machine can take any potentially attractive pebble or small stone and smooth it till it has a permanent shine. You can tumble pebbles picked up from the beach or stones you have found in the countryside. Or, if you are not satisfied with what you have collected or want greater variety, you can buy rough pieces of stone from lapidary shops and polish them. The smoother the stone you start with, the shorter the process; but even rough pieces can be polished successfully. And the results are stones of beauty and fascination that you can use in all sorts of different ways.

Choosing a tumbler

A simple tumbling machine consists of a small barrel, which is turned by rollers, powered through a pulley or gear system by an electric motor. The stones are placed inside the barrel with just enough water to cover them and a small quantity of very hard grit, called silicon carbide. They then tumble on top of each other till they are smoothed down. Coarse grits are used at first, then finer grits and lastly a polishing agent.

There are tumbling kits available which usually include a machine, the necessary grits and polishing agents, a batch of stones, epoxy resin glue and a selection of findings or jewellery mounts, to which you attach your polished stones. Any shop specializing in lapidary will stock all the equipment you need—they are quite used to giving guidance to beginners so don't be put off by the fact that they also deal in finished stones and supplies for experts.

Tumbling machines are available in a variety of sizes and with one or more barrels. Most small machines run at one speed only but some offer variable speeds.

Machines with two or more barrels are very useful, since you can tumble different sets of stones at the same time. This avoids the bother of having to wait till one cycle is completed before starting another. It is ideal, too, if you can keep one barrel exclusively for the final polish since, for this, the barrel must be completely free of grit. In small barrels you can only tumble stones up to about 4cm. (1½in.), therefore a larger barrel means that you can tumble larger stones.

With a variable-speed machine you can shorten the first, rough tumbling stage by using the high speed. The low speed (standard for one-speed machines) is used for the later stages, when fast tumbling will cause cracking and unsatisfactory results.

The disadvantage of larger or more complicated machines is that they cost more. If you intend to make jewellery in commercial quantities they are well worth the extra cost, but the beginner will probably be satisfied with a small machine.

Small, one-speed machines usually have a capacity of 675g. (1½lb.) to 1.35kg. (3lb.) and are able to tumble 100-200 pebbles at a time, from the size of a pea up to roughly the size of the top joint of your thumb. With the larger machines you can tumble slightly larger stones.

The smoothing grits used in tumbling machines are made of silicon carbide. This is much harder than any pebble, with a hardness of 9½ on Mohs' scale, and makes an excellent abrasive for smoothing pebbles.

The grits are distinguished by grade numbers—the higher the grade number, the finer the grit. '60 grade' grit, which is commonly used for grinding the rough edges off pebbles, will pass through a screen with 60 meshes per 2.5cm. (1in.) Grits from

A basic machine for tumbling and polishing stones.

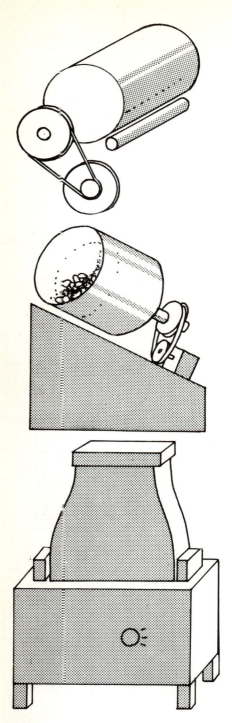

Three types of tumblers **Top**
*horizontal barrel (where one or more
barrels rotate on horizontal rollers);*
Centre *inclined barrel (one that is
closed at one end and attached to an
inclined spindle); and* **Bottom** *vibro
tumbler (where one or more hoppers
is attached to a platform vibrating at
2500 vibrations per minute.*

60 grade to 600 grade, which
roughly corresponds to the difference between coarse sandpaper and
fine glasspaper, are available at any
rock shop.

Polishing agents are used in the
final tumbling stage. These are
tin oxide (putty powder) or cerium
oxide and are used to add the polish
when a stone is already smooth.

Making your own tumbler

Unless materials are readily available you should not expect to save
money by constructing a home-made
machine. A 'one-off' machine is
always more expensive than one of
a batch. The reward comes at the
end of the process, when you see a
pile of beautiful glossy stones produced by a machine built and run
by you.

Barrels: The first thing to decide is
the size of the barrel. A larger barrel
taking, say, 3kg.(6lb.) works effi-
ciently because the heavier weight
of stone gives more rapid grinding.
But do you have any use for large
quantities of stones? Taking quartz
materials, eg tigers-eye, rose quartz,
amethyst, agate, etc (which are
among the most popular), pendant
size pieces of the order of 4cm. ×
2·5cm.($\frac{1}{2}$in. × 1in.) would run at 30 to
40 to the half kilo for the finished
stones, while smaller stones say
1·3cm. × 1·3cm.($\frac{1}{2}$in. × $\frac{1}{2}$in.) suitable
for bracelets, cuff-links and neck-
laces would be around 350–400 per
half kilo. Smaller machines taking a
charge of 675g–1kg.(1$\frac{1}{2}$–2lb.) of stone
are easier to move and also quieter
in operation.

The following considerations are
therefore based on a barrel size of
diameter 11·3cm.(4$\frac{1}{2}$in.) and width
6·3cm.(2$\frac{1}{2}$in.) which will accommodate about 675g.(1$\frac{1}{2}$lb.) of stone
(fig. 1, opposite page). Such barrels
are available from rock shops.

Base board: The machine will be
constructed to accommodate two
barrels, one for grinding and one for
polishing. The framework could be
of metal but most people would find
it easier to construct this in wood.
The base board must be large enough
to mount the meter as well as the
spindles. A suggested size would be
30cm. × 12·5cm. × 2cm.(12in. × 5in.
× $\frac{3}{4}$in.). Rubber pads or feet must be
fixed on the bottom of the base
board to minimize noise.

Spindles and bearings: The
spindles should be about 20cm.

Chrysoprase

Rhodonite

Rose Quartz

Snowflake Obsidian

Crocidolite (Tiger Eye)

Mookaite

Amethyst

Tree Agate

Red Jasper

Moss-Agate

Cornelian

Rhyolite

(8in.) in length and, say, 0·8cm.–1·3cm.($\frac{3}{8}$–$\frac{1}{2}$in.) in diameter. The bearings may be simple bronze bushes which can be obtained already impregnated with graphite and oil. 'Plummer' blocks with ball races are also available and would be an improvement but are about ten times the price. The end boards for the bearings may be of the same material as the base board and should be shaped and drilled to give a firm screw fixing to the base board. It is essential that the spindles be mounted parallel, therefore drill the holes for the bearings with the two end boards clamped together. The distance between the hole centres should be about two-thirds the diameter of the barrel. The drive spindle should protrude far enough to allow the pulley to be attached. A modification would be to drive the free running shaft by letting both shafts protrude at the far end and run a rubber band between the two. Both spindles may be covered with rubber or plastic tubing to give better traction on the side of the barrels. If tubing of different thickness is used on one half of the spindles then it is possible to run two barrels at different speeds at the same time. To cut down friction place greased steel washers at either end of the spindles between the end boards and rubber sleeves, and recess magnetic ball bearings into the end boards (fig. 2).

Speeds of tumbling barrels
Each diameter of barrel has an optimum speed of rotation to produce best results. At this speed the pieces of rough are carried up the side of the barrel to a point where they 'flop over' and slide back in a layer to the bottom of the barrel (fig. 3). If the speed is too fast the stones are carried too high and fall back rather than sliding, which causes chipping and cracking.
If the speed is much too high the stones are carried right over by centrifugal action with little or no abrasive effect. Too slow speeds extend processing times and tend to give flattened stones. The correct speed is indicated by a low murmuring accompanied by a continuous swishing noise. As a rough guide the following are recommended ranges of speeds.

barrel dia.	revs/min.
10cm.(4in.)	45–55

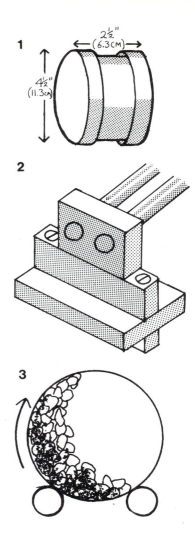

15cm.(6in.)	35–50
20cm.(8in.)	30–40

The standard speed of an electric motor on 50 cycle mains is 1420 rpm. Therefore a reduction of approximately 6 to 1 is needed, say 2·5cm. (1in.) on the motor and 15cm.(6in.) pulley on the spindle. A slower speed of say 30–35 rpm gives a more gentle action during the polishing stage and this is easily achieved by putting a smaller pulley on the motor or a larger pulley on the spindle. Slots in the base board allow adjustment of the motor to maintain tension in the vee belt. Only light belts are required and they should not be made too tight because this places unnecessary strain on the bearings.

Running a tumbler

When your tumbling machine is operating, it will run twenty-four hours a day for up to three weeks at a time—and it will be very noisy. Therefore you must put it somewhere where it will not be in the way and where there is a power point (electrical outlet).

The stones tumbling over each other make a continuous swishing noise, so the tumbler should not be located where noise will be a nuisance. A workshop away from the house is ideal but a little-used corner away from bedrooms will do.

If you put the machine on top of several layers of newspaper, this will help to deaden the sound and also to catch any dirt that may spill when you load or unload the machine. A strong cardboard box, with one end open for ventilation, also acts as an effective sound barrier.

Operating the tumbler

Before you load the machine, check the pebbles you are going to use—they should be of varying sizes and of similar hardness (see Mohs' scale on page 26).

The smaller stones 'fit in' to the angles of the larger ones, so that more of their surface is being rubbed at any one time. Softer stones will rapidly be worn away by the harder ones, become ruined and clog up the whole process. Try to make a batch of pebbles in a similar condition— if there are some which are much more pitted than others, they will inevitably need more rough tumbling.

Load the barrel three-quarters full of appropriate pebbles. Pour in water till it just covers them. Add coarse silicon carbide grit according to the manufacturer's instructions —a tablespoonful of 60 grade grit is about right for a 675g. (1½lb.) barrel.

Make sure that the lid of the barrel fits tightly, place the barrel on the rollers and switch on the motor. The barrel should turn smoothly at about 40 revolutions per minute and the sound of the pebbles should be an even, swishing rumble.

If the sound is uneven and clicking noises can be heard, check your load. You may have too few pebbles, or some that are too large; if it sounds as if there is little movement going on, you may have too many. In time, you will know immediately by the sound coming from the tumbler if the operation is going well.

The first rough-grind stage will continue for 5-7 days; exactly how long depends on the hardness and initial smoothness of the pebbles. The rough-grind cycle is finished when the grit has been completely worn into clay. Inspect the load daily. You will not see too much difference in the first day or two, so replace any stones you took out, seal the lid and continue tumbling. Many stones contain small quantities of gas, which are released as the surfaces of the stones are ground away. These small quantities may build up if you do not remove the lid once in every twenty-four hours.

When the grit has been worn away, empty the whole load through a strainer into a bucket half filled with water. Let the sludge sink to the bottom and then wash as much grit as possible off the pebbles by dunking the strainer in the water at the top of the bucket. Finally, rinse the pebbles in running water and let them dry on a soft cloth.

If there is clean water at the top of the bucket, you may pour it off but do *not* let any of the sludge go down the drain—you will block it. The sludge dries like cement. Empty the sludge into a plastic bag, which can be sealed and thrown away.

The second rough-grind cycle. If you are working with rounded beach pebbles, already partly smoothed by wave action, the rough-grind stage may only need one cycle. However, if you are using

This tumbling machine has two barrels so that stones of two hardnesses can be polished at the same time.

jagged, broken gemstones from a rock face, you may need three complete rough-grind cycles to achieve a good shape. In that case, repeat the operation with clean barrel, water and grit.

Eventually, the surface roughness will have been worn away, at least from most of the batch. At this stage sort the stones. Any that are still badly marked should be held back for re-tumbling with your next batch. The stones that are ready for the next stage will have an opaque look when dry but should be free of rough edges or obvious imperfections.

Second stage tumbling. Rinse the barrel thoroughly. Any particles of grit that remain will interfere with the finer grinding to come.

Replace the pebbles. If you have had to discard many, you may have to rough-grind another load before moving on to this stage. The barrel should be more than two-thirds full and, once again, too few pebbles will give a bad result. Load the barrel as before, using a finer grit (200 grade) and repeat the procedure, inspecting daily until the grit is worn away. This stage should remove the roughness left after the first stage.

When this is done, after a few days' tumbling, clean the barrel and pebbles as before, using the sludge-collecting method described in the first stage to avoid blocking the drains.

Fine grinding. Re-load and repeat the operation, using very fine silicon carbide grit (600 grade). Tumble for 5—7 days. Keep checking the load daily, until the surface of the pebbles is perfectly smooth and has a semi-gloss finish.

It is essential at this stage that you clean everything thoroughly—the pebbles, the barrel and the lid. If there are any grains of grit left, you will fail to achieve a high polish. Check the stones again and reject any that are cracked. Be absolutely ruthless about this; cracked stones will cause scratches on the others. Re-tumble them with your next load before polishing them.

The final polish. Put the selected pebbles back into the clean barrel carefully, so they do not chip each other as they fall. Add clean water to cover them. Add polishing powder, according to the manufacturer's instructions—a teaspoonful of tin oxide or cerium oxide should be right for a 675g. ($1\frac{1}{2}$lb.) machine.

If, when you start tumbling, sharp noises indicate that the pebbles are rattling unevenly against each other, you may add a teaspoonful of wallpaper glue to thicken the mixture, but do not use too much. Clean plastic pellets, which are available at rock shops, make a good filler if you do not have quite a full load.

Check the pebbles daily, as before. It will probably be about four days before they show a good gleam but keep going until there is no noticeable improvement on the day before. There is a perfect polish when the pebbles shine as brilliantly when they are dry as when they are wet.

Clean the barrel and rinse off the stones. Sometimes, the polish can be improved by tumbling for a few hours with a few drops of detergent in water. Be careful not to use too much detergent, or the bubbles will force the lid off. Finally, rinse and dry the stones. They should now have a sparkle which they will never lose.

Hints on tumbling

Remember the quality of stones coming out of your tumbler will only be as good as the material you put in. Therefore reject poor grade rough and material with cracks, pores, soft inclusions and deep cavities. *Always wear gloves and goggles when breaking up rocks to protect against sharp splinters.* A short time spent grinding off poor areas and awkward shapes is repaid by shorter tumbling times and consequently less loss of good material. Also bear in mind that pre-form shapes eg beads, cabochons and hearts may be finished in tumblers.

Reserve a barrel for polishing only and mark it and the lid clearly. Many different powders have been used for polishing but those most favoured are tin oxide (putty powder) and cerium oxide. Some people find that small squares of materials ('polishers') such as wood, cork or leather help polishing.

Some operators add a little polycell to the polishing mixture and some manufacturers sell tablets to thicken the polishing slurry.

General hints

The barrel or barrels rotate horizontally on rollers which should

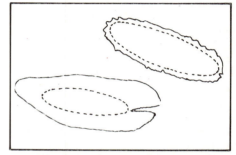

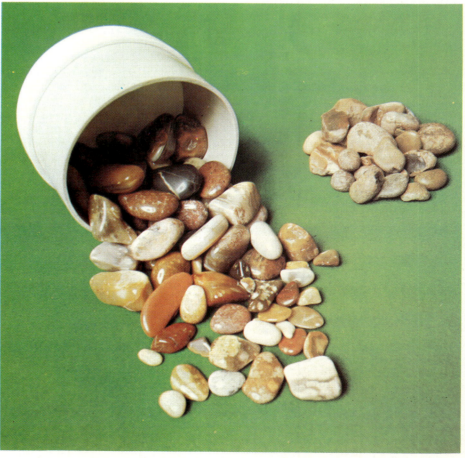

Right *Pebbles or stones with deep cracks are not worth keeping; too much is lost in the tumbling process.* **Below** *The vivid contrast between unpolished and polished stones.*

rotate easily by hand. If they do not the motor has to overcome friction and will consequently run hot and use more electricity.

The steel rollers are usually covered with plastic or rubber tubing to grip the sides of the barrels. Bearings may be plain bushes or of roller or ball type. Many different sizes and types of barrels have been used from round to hexagonal or octagonal cross-section, with one end permanently closed like a bottle or jar, or with removable caps at each end to facilitate cleaning. The important points are that they should be easy to seal and leakproof, but easy to unseal at regular intervals to release gas pressure. The barrel interior should be smooth and free from crevices that would trap grit, making it difficult to clean out between stages.

Metal barrels are noisy and prone to wear unless lined with rubber or plastic sheeting. Glass jars should *never* be used because of explosion hazards. Plastic bottles are easy to obtain and they work well, but a narrow neck restricts the size of the stones that may be processed. The best answer is to use a plastic jar with sealable lid or a plastic tube with caps at both ends.

One roller is driven by an electric motor via belt and pulleys, the other may be free running. The motor size depends on the size and number of barrels but it will be in the range $\frac{1}{16}$th to $\frac{1}{4}$ horse power. Small sewing machine type motors are often used. All motors must be continuous rated, because they will have to run for periods of weeks at a time with only short inspection breaks.

It is a good idea to keep a record of exactly how long you have taken over each stage and exactly what materials and quantities you have used. Keep a couple of stones untumbled from each batch, so you can compare them with the final result and refer to them later, when you have a similar batch to work with.

Don't be afraid to experiment with different grades of grit or varying lengths of time—different stones will need slightly different procedures and even the experts are continually experimenting! You should be able to get an impressive result first time but, as always, there is no substitute for practical experience.

Stones for tumbling
grouped according to Mohs' scale

Below is a list of the stones most commonly available through rock shops which are suitable for tumbling.

You will notice that some stones range over two or three numbers, such as serpentine $2\frac{1}{2}$-4. This is because some stones have different hardness values, depending on what part of the world they come from. Always test them before mixing with other stones in your tumbler. Add to this list the Mohs' scale number of other stones you find or buy.

8	Beryl 8	Topaz 8
	Chrysoberyl $8\frac{1}{2}$	
7	Most Agates $7\frac{1}{2}$	Jadeite $6\frac{1}{2}$-7
	Agatized Coral $7\frac{1}{2}$	Jasper 6-7
	Amethyst 7	Mookaite $7\frac{1}{2}$
	Bloodstone 7	Moroccan Beans $7\frac{1}{2}$
	Chalcedony $7\frac{1}{2}$	Petrified Wood 7
	Crocidolite (Tiger Eye) 7	Petrified Bone 7
	Cornelian $7\frac{1}{2}$	Pink Botswana $7\frac{1}{2}$
	Chrysoprase 7	Quartz Crystal 7
	Citrine 7	Rock Crystal 7
	Chalcedony Onyx 7	Rose Quartz 7
	Flint $7\frac{1}{2}$	Rutilated Quartz 7
	Garnet $7\frac{1}{2}$	Smoky Quartz 7
	Green Garnet 7	Tourmaline $7\frac{1}{2}$
	Greek Chalcedony $7\frac{1}{2}$	Turitella Agate 6-7
	Iolite 7	Zircon $7\frac{1}{2}$
6	Amazonite 6	Magnetite 6
	Aventurine 6-$6\frac{1}{2}$	Opal 6
	Black Jade $6\frac{1}{2}$	Prehnite 6-$6\frac{1}{2}$
	Bruneau Jasper $6\frac{1}{2}$	Pyrite 6
	Chrysocolla 5-$7\frac{1}{2}$	Rhodonite $5\frac{1}{2}$-$6\frac{1}{2}$
	Green Jade $6\frac{1}{2}$	Rutile 6-$6\frac{1}{2}$
	Hematite $5\frac{1}{2}$	Sodalite 6
	Jadeite $6\frac{1}{2}$-7	Sunstone 6
	Jasper 6-7	Turitella Agate 6-7
	Labradorite 6	Turquoise 4-6
5	Apatite 5	Nephrite $5\frac{1}{2}$
	Brazilianite $5\frac{1}{2}$	Obsidian 5
	Chrysocolla 5-$7\frac{1}{2}$	Rhyolite 5-6
	Moonstone 5	Turquoise 4-6
4	Bowenite 4	Serpentine $2\frac{1}{2}$-4
	Fluorite 4	Turquoise 4-6
3	Aragonite 3	Limestone 3
	Calcite Onyx $3\frac{1}{2}$	Malachite $3\frac{1}{2}$
	Coral $3\frac{1}{2}$	Marble 3-$3\frac{1}{2}$
	Jet 3	Serpentine $2\frac{1}{2}$-4
2	Alabaster 2	Serpentine $2\frac{1}{2}$-4
	Amber 2-$2\frac{1}{2}$	

Cabochons & Faceting

The cutting and polishing of gem stones may be divided into two broad categories: those styles with curved surfaces, eg beads, cabochons, carvings, cameos, intaglios and baroque shapes, and those styles using flat facets.

The earliest, simplest and cheapest method of fashioning gemstones is simply to polish the surface of the 'rough' (uncut gemstone), more or less retaining the original shape. A classical example of this is the Black Prince's Ruby (really a fine red spinel), which is around 5cm. (2in.) long, of polished irregular shape and is in the British Imperial State Crown. Although originally this style of cutting was done by hand, these days it is more usual to use the tumbling process which yields highly polished baroque stones with irregular contours.

Carved stones such as figures, objects, snuff bottles, cameos, intaglios and seal stones which have a history going back thousands of years are still being produced.

Although the process has been speeded up by using electric power tools and diamond points, the procedure is still a lengthy one re-quiring much patience and artistic skill.

Cabochons

Probably the most widely used style of curved cut stones is the cabochon. A simple cabochon is a polished stone with a rounded top surface and a regular outline. Cabochons are made in a wide range of materials and shapes, their outlines may be oval, round, drop or heart shape and the top may have a high, medium or low dome. The back of the stone may have a similar curvature to that of the front, or it may be flat with a small bevel round the periphery, and it may be polished or left semi-polished or matte. Cabochons are even produced with the back hollowed out to lighten the colour of a dark stone. The Almandine garnet 'carbuncles' much used in Victorian jewellery were such stones.

Although precious stones such as emeralds, rubies and sapphires were formerly cut 'en cabochon', the style is now reserved for precious stones not 'clean' enough to warrant faceting, or for translucent or opaque stones such as jade, coral, agate, turquoise and opal. It is also

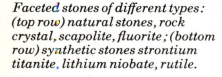

Faceted stones of different types: (top row) natural stones, rock crystal, scapolite, fluorite; (bottom row) synthetic stones strontium titanite, lithium niobate, rutile.

used to bring out optical effects in some stones, eg chrysoberyl 'cats-eyes' and corundum star stones.

Faceted stones

Faceting was probably first introduced to enhance the surface reflection and give more interesting shapes. Records show that in the early Middle Ages diamond octahedra had their natural faces polished to give 'point stones', and some small diamonds with random facets are still seen in jewellery. The next development was to grind off one corner of a diamond octahedron and to polish the flat facet to give a 'table-cut'. It was gradually realized that faceting could reveal all the hidden fire in diamonds and around 1670 Peruzzi of Venice was given credit for developing the full brilliant cut. This cut, consisting of 33 facets above the girdle and 24 facets below (25 if a culet is cut), became the accepted style for diamond cutting and has remained the most popular style to the present day. It is particularly suitable for colourless stones of high refractive index and dispersion eg diamond and zircon, because it reveals the full fire (ability to split light into rainbow colours) of such stones. The brilliant cut is also successfully used for coloured stones such as ruby, sapphire, blue and golden zircons, red and green garnets and tourmalines.

Some of the factors which the lapidary must take into account are as follows. Coloured rough stone should be oriented to show best colour through the top, because this is the usual direction from which stones are viewed. The facets must be accurately placed and polished to a high degree of flatness to achieve maximum brilliancy. The pavilion facets must be arranged to behave like miniature mirrors, reflecting back through the crown the maximum amount of incident light. The angle which the pavilion facets make with the girdle is critical to produce the desired total internal reflection. The correct angle varies from one gem species to another depending on the refractive index (R.I.) but it is around 40° and in general the lower the R.I. of the stone the deeper it must be cut.

It is also necessary to take into account directions of easy cleavage and flaws, fractures, variation in hardness and brittleness. Often a compromise has to be made when encountering an awkwardly shaped piece of rough or when the colour is so deep or so pale that ideal proportions are not practicable.

There are a great many variations on the brilliant cut, including double brilliants for large stones, marquise or navette (boat shaped), the pendalogue (tear shaped), oval and cushion shaped.

Another important style of faceting is the step or trap cut. This cut is most suitable for stones which rely mainly on colour for their beauty. It consists basically of a four-sided table facet with four-sided oblong facets cut parallel to its edges. The

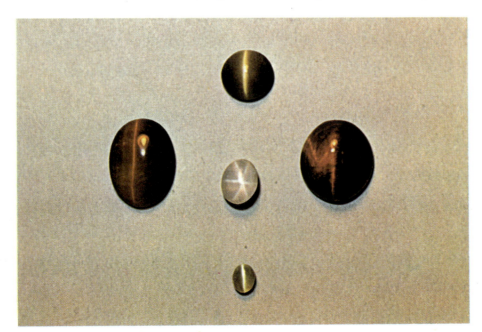

Polished cabochons showing chatoyancy (cat's eye effect) and asterism (star effect). Top quartz cat's eye middle red tiger's eye, sapphire star stone and yellow tiger's eye, and bottom chrysoberyl cat's eye.

37

rectangular style with the four corners truncated to give an eight-sided stone, is so often used for the beautiful velvety green emerald that it has become known as the 'emerald cut'. The angles needed to produce total internal reflection are still important, but the depth of colour is probably the overriding factor. Deep

coloured stones will need a shallow profile to allow light through them, while pale stones will be cut deeply to enhance their colour.

Many variations of the step cut are in use including baguette (long rectangular), kite, lozenge, keystone, hexagonal and octagonal. Many stones are produced with a 'mixed cut', for example a brilliant crown and step cut pavilion.

Cutting and polishing processes and equipment

Since many of the preliminary processes are common to the production of both cabochons and faceted stones they may be dealt with together.

Slabbing. Many gemstones occur in quite large masses of rough, eg agates, jades and lapis lazuli and so the first process is to reduce them to workable sized slabs by cutting with a slabbing saw. This type of saw consists of a metal disc with its circumference impregnated with diamond grit, revolving at several hundred revolutions per minute, while being cooled by water or oil. The diameter of slabbing saws varies from, say, 20cm.(8in.) to a metre or several feet and the correct speed of revolution depends on the diameter. The greater the diameter the slower the speed must be.

The slab is inspected and the desired area selected for colour or pattern and freedom from cracks and faults.

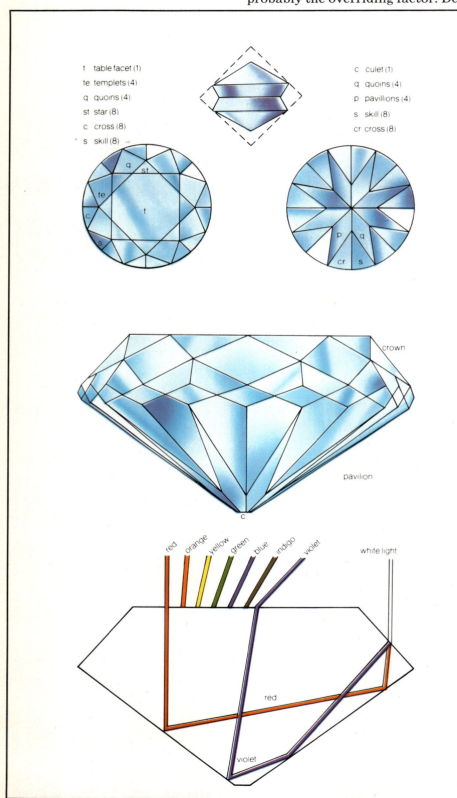

t	table facet (1)	c	culet (1)
te	templets (4)	q	quoins (4)
q	quoins (4)	p	pavillions (4)
st	star (8)	s	skill (8)
c	cross (8)	cr	cross (8)
s	skill (8)		

Unwanted areas of stone are removed on a trim saw, a smaller version of the slabbing saw.

If the stone is to be a cabochon its outline may be drawn at this stage, using a plastic template and an aluminium pencil. Ordinary pencils or felt tip pens are not of much use since the mark easily gets washed away or rubbed off. It should be noted that the outline is drawn on the base and the best side of the slab should be reserved for the top. Faceting rough usually only occurs in small pieces and a thin blade in the trim saw is sufficient to trim off unwanted areas without too much waste.

Grinding
This process employs vertically revolving wheels of silicon carbide of about 15–25cm.(6–10in.) diameter with water cooling. In some professional cutting centres sandstone wheels of up to a metre or several feet in diameter are used. There are also automatic machines which mechanically produce pre-forms and these probably have diamond impregnated grinding wheels. Most amateurs use a 15–20cm.(6–8in.) combination machine, consisting of a coarse grinding wheel (100 grit), a fine grinding wheel (220 grit) and an attachment for a disc sander or polishing lap.

The trim sawed cabochon blank is profiled on the coarse grinding wheel using a steadying rest, keeping the aluminium outline uppermost. The blank is swept from side to side to make smooth curves (and to wear the grindstone down evenly), until a uniform border is left about 0·15cm.($\frac{1}{16}$in.) wide. If the aluminium mark is ground away the stone will end up undersize and it will be difficult to maintain the correct shape. A tiny 45° bevel is then ground on the base of the stone just up to the profile mark, which reduces the tendency to chip and also makes the finished stone easier to set.

The cabochon blank is then fixed on a dop stick to make handling easier. Dop sticks are hardwood dowels of 10–12·5cm.(4–5in.) in length and of a range of diameters say from 0·3–2cm. ($\frac{1}{8}$–$\frac{3}{4}$in.). Special dopping wax is available but stick shellac also works well. Dopping is carried out by warming the stone over a spirit lamp or hot plate, a fragment of shellac on the stone's surface indicates by melting when the temperature is right. Some stones are heat sensitive and will crack or shatter if allowed to get too hot. A suitably sized dop stick with a coating of shellac or wax on the end is warmed in the flame and attached to the back of the stone. While the wax is still soft the stone is centred on the dop stick and the wax moulded with the fingers to give good support; it is then put down to cool.

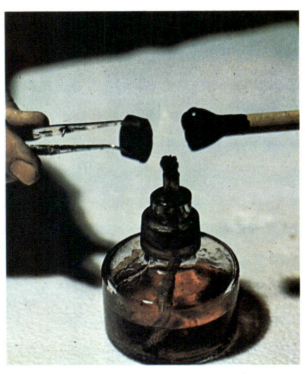

Far Left *How brilliant-cut diamonds come from a stone. Cleavages, maccles and flats are less regular fragments. The diagram also shows three views of a brilliant: the crown or top part has 33 facets and the pavilion or lower part has 24 or 25. The brilliant cut gives most 'fire' to a diamond because it is proportioned to reflect all the colours into which an entering ray of white light is split. The diagram indicates how such light is refracted, split and reflected.*
Below Left *A diamond edged slabbing saw cutting a piece of rough agate. The machine has a mechanical feed which pushes the rough against the blade to 'slice' the slabs.*
Below Right *Dopping the pre-form to the dop stick. Heat from the burner melts the wax on the dop stick and warms the stone, held by forceps, which is then fixed to the wax. The pre-form is then ground to the required shape.*

Some popular cabochon cuts **Top** *high cabochon* **First from Top** *medium cabochon* **Second from Top** *low cabochon* **Below** *hollow cabochon.*

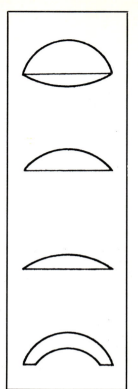

The next step is to rough-grind the top of the stone by cutting a series of bevels starting at the girdle with a bevel sloping in about 10–15° towards the centre. The aim should be to preserve the outline with smooth curves until the top of the stone is reached. Care must be taken not to leave a flat spot at the top of the stone.

Fine grinding is carried out with the 220 grit wheel that has been well dressed for smooth grinding. The whole surface is smoothed to remove all scratches left from the rough grinding. Don't give in to the temptation to proceed to sanding too soon, since all the shaping should be done at the grinding stage. Pre-forms for faceted gems are best made on the 220 wheel. First the top of the stone is decided upon and then ground flat (the side of the wheel is useful to finish on). Next the outline of the stone, round for brilliant or rectangular for step cut, is marked in Indian ink and protected with liquid shellac or nail varnish. For step cut stones the depth should equal the width and the girdle is marked about a third down from the top. A circular brilliant pre-form may be ground by hand or the rough may be dopped and the pre-form ground on the faceting machine to give a very much more symmetrical gem.

Sanding

Sanding of cabochons is carried out on waterproof cloth discs or discs of wet or dry paper which are stuck with rubber based adhesive to a metal disc. Sometimes a sponge rubber backing is used to help produce smooth curves. Plenty of water should be used to remove cutting debris and keep the stone cool. Beginning at the sides and proceeding to the top to which special attention should be paid, the stone is completely sanded using sweeping and rocking movements, first on 220 grit then on 400 grit discs. It is not necessary to sand pre-forms for faceting.

Polishing cabochons

It is almost true to say that there are as many polishing techniques as there are lapidaries. Each person develops his own preference and each gem material requires a different combination of lap and powder. Laps in common use are hard felt, leather, wood, non-woven fibre cloths and plastics. Polishing powders include the old-fashioned rotten stone (natural earthy material), aluminium oxide (ruby powder and linda A), silica powder (tripoli), iron oxide, tin oxide (putty powder) and cerium oxide. Diamond grits down to 0·1 micron are also used and particularly recommended on wood for

ruby and sapphire star stones.

Felt laps used with cerium oxide will polish cabochons of the quartz family quicker and better than most combinations, and hard leather on a wood or metal backing with linda A is a good combination for polishing most gem stones.

Most powders are used suspended in water as a creamy paste and most laps polish best just as they are about to dry out. At this point the lap begins to squeak and tug on the cabochon. The polishing action is rapid but considerable heat is generated and care must be taken not to melt the wax or crack the stone.

Finally the stone is removed from the dop by warming carefully over a spirit flame until the wax softens. Then clean in warm solvent eg methylated spirits (denatured alcohol).

Cutting and polishing faceted stones

Cutting and polishing faceted stones are complicated, technical processes, and should not be attempted by the amateur until he has acquired some expertise. Since they are, however, essential to the practice of gemology, a brief explanation of the processes follows. Basically the faceting pre-forms have the facets cut by holding them against horizontal revolving laps. It is essential to get the facets on the stone in the right place and at the correct angle. Professional cutters achieve this result by the traditional 'jamb peg' method. This is a block of wood covered in small round depressions into which the sharpened back end of the dop stick is located. By choosing the correct hole the angle is controlled and the facet cut. It is all done by hand and eye, and considerable skill and practice is required. However modern faceting machines as used by most amateurs and some professionals, have faceting heads which set the correct angles and alignment by the use of notched gear wheels and angle quadrants. Most of these types of machine are capable of giving very accurate results with the minimum of skill. Each set of facets has a particular elevation angle and each individual facet corresponds to a numbered notch on the gear wheel. Providing the step by step instructions are followed an acceptable gem must result.

The process may be illustrated by describing the cutting of a standard brilliant from quartz. The pre-form is mounted on a metal dop stick and then locked in the 45° attachment; this allows the table to be cut. Copper laps with diamond impregnated, or cast iron laps with loose silicon carbide may be used. The dop is then locked in the dop arm which is set to 40° and the two crown main (or bezel facets) corresponding to notches 32 and 64 are cut. These are followed by nos 16 and 48 and then 8, 24, 40 and 56 till all 8 bezel facets are cut. Next the facet head is raised and set in an angle 15° less than the main angle of 40° ie 25° and the 8 star facets are cut in. The head is then lowered and the arm set at 40° + 3° and the 16 skill (or upper girdle) facets are cut. The procedure is then repeated for polishing, using say tin oxide on a tin lap. The stone is then clamped in a transfer jig and carefully re-dopped on a second dop stick, this time with the base or pavilion exposed.

The most critical part is lining up the first pair of pavilion facets with a corresponding pair on the crown. Once this has been done the angle is set at 43° assuming a quartz gem is being cut and the 8 pavilion mains are cut, followed by the 16 lower girdle facets in a similar manner to the crown. Polishing is again carried out in a similar manner to the crown.

Jewellery making

Once you have polished stones, the next step is to use them. Stones can be made very simply into attractive —and unique—pieces of jewellery by using commercially available mountings, which are called 'findings'.

Findings are sold in lapidary shops and many craft shops which also sell polished stones, if you want to make jewellery but are not interested in polishing stones yourself.

Findings are made in various metals, at varying prices—the beginner is wise to start with cheap metal ones but, when you have made a few pieces, you may want to set a special stone in silver or gold. This is no more difficult, but do remember that the beauty of the stones is usually best shown off by simple settings.

Essentially, jewellery is made by gluing the stones to findings. There are three basic types of jewellery findings—flat pads, to which stones with flat bases are glued; bell caps which are bent over an end of a stone (usually a pear-shaped one); and claw settings where you glue a stone to a base and bend adjustable 'claws' round the stone to hold it in position.

These three types cover the findings you glue to the stone. Other findings include jump rings which are used to connect one section (notably, bell caps) to another. You can buy bracelets or necklets which may have flat pads or claws, others may need jump rings and bell caps to attach the stones. In general, you can buy findings for use as ear-rings, pendants, brooches, cuff-links, key rings—almost any piece of jewellery you may want to make—using one or other of the three methods.

The right finding for each stone. What finding you use depends on the stone and what you intend to do with it and this is discussed in more detail later in the chapter.

Equipment
You will need:

Polished stones.
Findings.
Epoxy resin adhesive.
Saucer for mixing adhesive.
Match-sticks for applying adhesive.
Jewellery pliers or tweezers.
Spirit.
Clean rags.
Shallow tray or tin.
Salt or sand.

Preparing stones and findings. Wash the stones and findings in warm water and detergent, to remove all traces of dirt and grease. Rinse and dry them thoroughly. Even the natural oils from fingers may affect adhesion, so a final wipe over with spirit is a good idea.

☐ Mix the epoxy resin, according to the manufacturer's instructions. Epoxy resin has the advantage of being extremely strong when it is set; but it is correspondingly difficult to remove, so be careful not to let any unwanted traces go hard.

☐ Since the resin takes time to set (up to three days for complete hardening), you may have to hold the stone and finding in position. To do this, pour a quantity of salt, sand or rice into a tray or tin and support them with this. Push the band of a ring or back of a brooch into the sand, so that the surface to be glued stays clear and level. If you are applying a bell cap to a stone, push the stone in and set the bell cap on it.

☐ Apply the resin with a match-stick to both the finding and the stone. Wipe off any unwanted blobs of glue with a clean rag.

☐ **With a 'claw' mount** bend the claws into position with jewellery pliers (tweezers will do) before inserting the stone. Pull them out of place as little as possible when inserting the stone and then bend them firmly over it.

☐ **With a bell cap** be careful to position the cap, by watching the position of the eyelet at the top of the cap, so that the face of the stone that you prefer will face outwards

when it hangs.

☐ When the glue is dry, brush off any particles of salt or sand from the finding and stone. If the piece needs to be connected to a chain or bracelet do this with a jump ring. Jewellery pliers will open these and twist them shut.

Part I—Findings

The last chapter described how to polish stones by tumbling, and the opening paragraphs of this chapter have discussed, in very general terms, how to bond your polished stones to metal mounts (called findings) to make finished articles of jewellery.

Continuing the theme that your tumbled stones (or bought polished stones) can be made into unique and lovely jewellery without any special knowledge of metal work, this section illustrates a representative cross-section of the findings to be found in lapidary and craft shops, and gives advice on deciding which findings are best suited to various sorts of stones.

Most shops sell findings for earrings, brooches, bracelets, necklaces, pendants, rings, tie clips and pins, and key rings—almost any jewellery you may want to make—in a variety of designs, sizes and different metals suitable for baroque (irregularly shaped) tumbled and polished stones.

Findings can be small and fine to complement delicate-looking small stones, or big and sturdy for large heavy stones. Styles vary from simple to ornate, and traditional to modern. Simple styles are easier to work on so it's wise to avoid ornate or filigree designs for your first attempt.

There is usually a choice of metals too—and prices vary accordingly. Some metal findings are very cheap indeed and, however attractive your stones, are liable to make the finished articles of jewellery look cheap and tatty too. Well made, handsome findings in base metals cost a little more but are worth paying for because they can transform the same tumbled stones into really elegant-looking pieces of jewellery. Brass and steel can be strong, and usually have a gilt or silver coloured finish. Stainless steel is also available for some types of findings, and you can choose either a brushed or polished finish. Sterling silver and 9ct. gold findings are considerably more expensive. It's no more difficult to set stones in these metals but it's obviously a good idea for the beginner to try her hand at jewellery making with the cheaper base metals first. Moreover, silver and gold findings are usually specifically designed to take the more expensive faceted stones and cabochons, and it may be difficult to find one which provides a suitably comfortable fit for a baroque tumbled stone.

The three basic findings

Whatever article of jewellery you are making, whether it be a pair of ear-rings or a bracelet, your stone will be bonded to one of three basic types of finding—bell cap, pad mount, or claw setting. The most fundamental factor in selecting the right finding lies in deciding which of these basic types is most suited to your stone—a decision which should be determined by the shape of the stone itself.

Bell caps

The majority of bell caps (fig.1) are very like their name, being bell-shaped in appearance. They have either four or seven prongs and provide the means for suspending a stone. They are frequently used for pendants, drop ear-rings, key rings and for attaching hanging stones to bracelets. Pear shaped, oblong or 'drop' stones that taper to a point are most suitable for these bell caps. The narrowest end of the stone is fitted into the cap, and it is positioned so that the most attractive facet of the stone faces outwards.

Another type of bell cap has two prongs only. Sometimes referred to as a leaf bail this is the finding to use for suspending a flat stone (fig.2).

Bonding a stone to a bell cap.

Choose a bell cap which is of complementary style and in proportionate size to your stone—and into which a corner of the stone will fit snugly. Always test and shape the cap on to the stone before bonding into position.

To ensure that the most attractive facet of the stone is visible in the finished piece of jewellery, turn the bell cap so that the eyelet hole is facing you, and insert the stone with its 'best' face towards you (fig.3). Press the stone down well, making sure that it touches the metal base of the cap. If necessary, lift back the

Right 1. Bellcaps, plain or ornate come in many sizes. 2. Leaf bails and jump rings also come in various sizes.
Far Right 3. Bellcap eyelet and the best facet of the stone should face you during bonding. To keep the best facet facing outwards, use one jump ring only to connect the bellcap to the chain (remember that jump rings interlock at 90° angles) or use any other odd number if you want extra length and 'dangle'. Never use an even number.

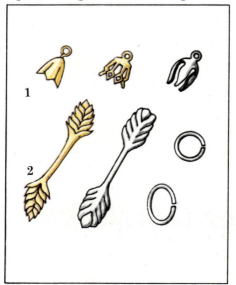

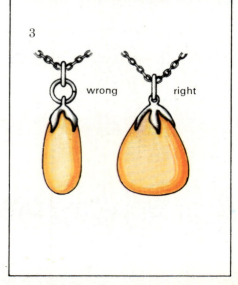

wrong   right

prongs a little with jewellery pliers or tweezers to seat them properly. Press the prongs firmly round the stone again to get the final effect.

Remove the stone and, providing you are satisfied that stone and cap are well suited, proceed to clean and glue both as described in the opening paragraphs of this chapter. The procedure for attaching a flat stone to a leaf bail type of bell cap

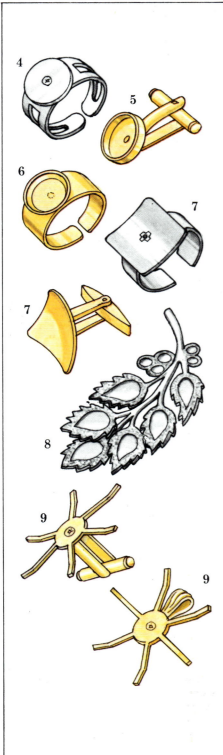

is very much the same. Again the question of proportionate size and complementary design should be taken into account. The finding is bent into a U shape the width of the stone. It is then bonded to the stone, leaving a deliberate gap between the top of the U and the stone itself in order to form an eyelet.

Jump rings

Having attached your stone to a bell cap, usually the next step is to pass a jump ring through the bell cap eyelet.

Jump rings (fig.2) are round or oval split rings of springy metal which act as connecting links to join one section of jewellery to another. They are used, for instance, for hanging a pendant on a neck chain, for drop ear-rings, and for suspending hanging stones from bracelets and key rings (fig.3).

Jump rings are not usually needed for putting a flat stone on to a chain necklet—providing the chain is slim, it can be threaded directly through the U-shaped space left between stone and leaf bail.

Key ring findings and most drop ear-ring findings already incorporate a jump ring on to which the bell cap can be directly threaded—so you don't need to add one.

To fix a jump ring. When your stone is firmly secured to its bell cap and the glue has thoroughly dried, open wide a suitable jump ring by twisting both ends of the ring sideways with two pairs of jewellery pliers. Now hook one end of the ring through the eyelet of the bell cap and, if it is to be hung on a loop or link (for an ear-ring, chain bracelet or necklet), thread the other end over the loop or through the link. Then close the jump ring by pinching together firmly with the pliers.

Pad mounts

A large number of ring, brooch,

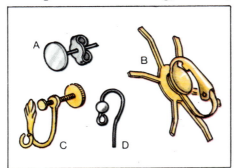

Far Left 4. Plain flat pad. 5. Flat pad with 90° angle raised edge intended for cabochons but, if large, it can take chippings. 6. Cup pad with flat base and gently raised edge and 7. concave pad with curved base are more suited to baroque stones. 8. Multipad takes several small stones. 9. Claw settings will grip awkwardly shaped stones.

Left 10. There are ear-ring findings for pierced and unpierced ears. Choose from (a) butterfly catch, (b) clip, (c) screw, and (d) hook fastenings. There are lots of styles in each category and each includes some pad mounts, claw settings and loops to take bellcap and stone.

Top Right *11. Base metal ring mounts fit any finger size. Different types of adjustable shanks as shown in these claw mounts, flat pad and concave flower pad rings.*

First from Top *12. Flat pads and claw mounts are most popular for cuff link findings.*

Second from Top *13. Tie pins, tie tacks and tie clips usually have flat pads.*

Top Far Right *14. Key rings with snake chain or mesh (see detail) take bellcaps.*

Below *15. Ready made chain bracelets and necklets come in many styles and sizes. Or you can buy a length of chain and a fastening (clasp and bolt ring are most common) and make up your own. Links can be large or small, round, oval, oblong, square or diamond shaped. In a trace chain the links interconnect at right angles. In a curb chain each link is twisted through 90° giving a 'flat look' finish.*

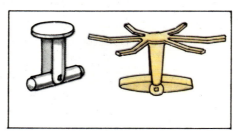

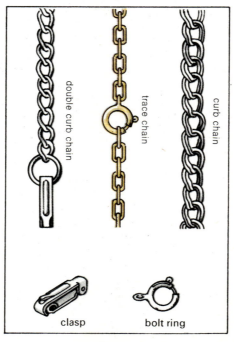

double curb chain

trace chain

curb chain

clasp

bolt ring

pendant, cuff-link, tie pin and earring findings incorporate a pad or pads on to which a stone or stones are able to be bonded.

Flat plain pads (fig.4) are probably the easiest for the beginner to use. This is the finding to choose for a stone that has a flat base, and an upper surface (the only part that will show in the completed piece of jewellery) that is attractive and interestingly shaped. Flat pads can be round, oval, square, oblong or triangular; and are available in a good choice of sizes.

It is always best to choose a pad that is as big as possible as this will give your stone maximum support, but remember that the pad must be just small enough to be completely concealed by the stone—or the results will be unsightly.

Large flat pads can be used for mounting a single stone or several smaller ones. Using several smaller stones is more tricky because it involves finding stones that harmonize in colour and shape. It also requires considerable care to ensure that the entire area of the pad will be covered. Moreover, because of their size, very small stones or chippings are difficult to handle—but this problem can be minimized by using tweezers or jewellery pliers when applying adhesive and seating the stones into their correct positions.

Flat pads with raised edges (fig. 5). Some flat pads—usually round or oval in shape—have raised edges or rims. This edge, which can be plain or decorated, rises at a 90° angle from the pads. These pads are ideal for use with cabochons and pre-formed stones and it is really preferable to reserve their use for these stones. Like all pad mounts they *can* be used for the more irregular shapes of tumbled and polished stones—but be warned that considerable perseverance and luck are needed to search out a suitable candidate stone from your own collection: it must be flat based and fit *precisely* into the area. They can also be used for chippings.

Cup pads (fig. 6) are a variation. Again you will have to take care to find a suitable stone but, because the edge rises gently at approximately 135° from the pad, the chances of finding a baroque or tumbled stone that fits well are considerably higher.

Concave pads are dished in varying depths, shapes and sizes to accommodate stones with gently rounded bases (fig.7). Again, it is best to choose a pad which is hidden by your stone but gives it maximum support. Small round filigree concave pads are sometimes called flower pads. They are so decorative that it doesn't matter if the stones fail to conceal the pads completely.

Multi-pads. Some findings, notably brooches and rings, incorporate several pads (fig.8). Often these consist of one large pad surrounded by several smaller pads. Or, sometimes, there are several pads of the same size. These are challenging for the jewellery maker intent on using her own tumbled stones because it takes time and patience to assemble stones that make a really attractive set—matching in size, colour and pattern. Moreover, many multi-pads are round or oval in shape and have raised edges— and these should definitely be reserved for use with cabochons and preformed stones only.

Claw settings

A claw setting is really a cross between a pad mount and a bell cap. It has a central pad on to which part of the stone is bonded, and claws or prongs which can be adjusted to close around the stone and hold it in position (fig.9). A claw setting is the most versatile of the three basic findings, and it can be used for a stone of almost any shape providing the stone has a small flattish area which can be bonded on to the pad. It is a very popular setting for rings, brooches and pendants, and increasingly used for cuff-link findings and other articles of jewellery too.

How to fit a claw mount. Choose a mount of size and style compatible with your stone. Place the stone on it, moving it around until you find the best position. If the stone has any definite bumps, it may be necessary to place each of the bumps between two claws to give a firm grip. Bend the claws gently round the stone with your fingers. Remove the stone and shape each claw with jewellery pliers, then replace the stone and complete the placement of the claws so that the stone is held in a fairly firm grip.

The stone can now be removed again, and the job of cleaning and bonding can begin. Remember that claws must be closely pressed against the stone or they will tend to catch in clothing.

Other jewellery findings

Ear-ring findings (fig.10) are made for pierced and unpierced ears. Check that ear wires are made of sterling silver or gold to avoid inflammation of delicate ear lobes. Drop ear-ring findings usually incorporate a loop on to which bell cap and stone can be threaded direct, but you can add jump rings if you wish to give extra 'dangle' and length.

Obviously, you will wish to spend time and care on selecting stones that look as though they belong together as a pair, but remember that no two stones are ever identical: compatibility of size, shape and colour should be your aim.

Ring mounts (fig.11). The majority of ring mounts have adjustable shanks which can simply be squeezed together to fit any finger. But sterling silver and 9ct. gold ring mounts are available in specific finger sizes. They need not be very costly and a silver ring with a flat pad can make an extremely handsome and durable mount for displaying a tumbled stone.

Cuff-links (fig.12), like ear-rings, require compatible stones. Because cuff-links take a lot of wear, it is particularly important to bond the stones very firmly. Scratching the surface of both stone and pad with a carborundum stone before cleaning and bonding ensures that the adhesive has a good surface to grip on (modern knife sharpeners are usually made of steel but if you have an old-fashioned one it is undoubtedly made of carborundum). Some decorative mounts have lacy filigree edges which can be bent over the stone with jewellery pliers for extra security.

Tie pins, tacks and clips (fig.13). Tie pins and tacks nearly always have a small round flat pad; and tie clips have a long narrow flat pad on to which a stone or row of stones can be mounted.

Key rings (fig.14) invariably incorporate a jump ring through which a bell cap and stone can be hung. Key rings are inclined to get a lot of wear, so it is advisable to use your carborundum stone on both stone and bell cap before bonding.

Chain bracelets and necklets (fig.15) can be bought ready made or can be made up by yourself. Trace chains consist of links joined at right angles to each other. In a curb chain each link is twisted through 90° so that the resulting chain has a 'flat look' finish. Chains can be bought purpose made for attaching pendants or hanging stones with bell caps and jump rings, or for threading directly through the gap between a flat stone and a leaf bail. A 67.5cm. (27in.) chain will slip over the head easily and is therefore a closed chain of links. Anything smaller than a 60cm. (24in.) chain will include a fastening. Alternatively, buy a length of chain and a fastening, and make the necklet or bracelet yourself. Try to purchase the exact length required. If you have to shorten a chain either open a link (as described for jump rings) and detach the unwanted extra length, or cut through closed metal links with silver shears. Never attempt to do the job with scissors as this will mangle both chain and scissors.

The most commonly available and simplest type of clasp is a bolt ring. Fit this spring loaded catch to one end of your chain, and a jump ring— on to which the bolt ring can engage—to the other end.

Bracelets and bangles (fig.16), like cuff-links, are subject to a lot of wear, so it's advisable to use a carborundum stone before applying adhesives.

The most usual kind of bracelet mount consists of flat pads joined by links. The pad can be of various shapes and there are usually six to eleven of them. Obviously the greater the number of pads, the more trouble it will take to assemble a set of stones of similar shape and size in harmonizing colours. Occasionally you will find a brace-

let mount with several chain links between each pad so that dangling stones can be interspersed with pad bonded stones.

Bangles are usually adjustable wide metal bands with a single large pad. Avoid pads with raised edges unless using chippings or a cabochon.

Pendants (fig.17). Basically there are two types of pendant findings, the simple and the ornate. The purpose of a simple pendant is purely to show off a stone. A claw setting falls into this category. So

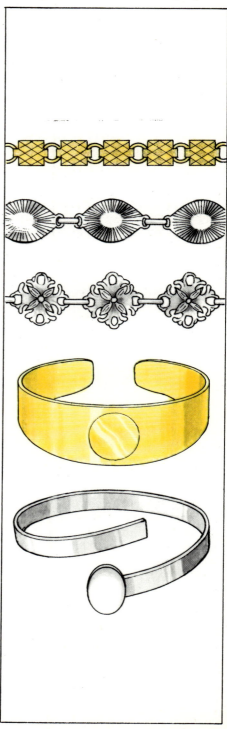

16. Bracelet and bangle findings usually have pad mounts. Some findings, such as the popular oval flat pad bracelet and the concave flower pad bracelet shown here, are very decorative in their own right so it does not matter if your stones fail to cover the pads completely.

does a small pad which will be completely concealed by the stone. But the majority of pendant findings are cast mountings and highly decorative in their own right. Available in every imaginable shape and design they incorporate a pad or pads on which a stone or stones can be mounted to complete the ornamentation.

Brooch mounts (fig.18) can be simple pin-backed pads on which a stone or stones can be mounted; or fob brooches (usually in a bow shape) with a loop from which a bell cap and stone can be hung; or decorative cast mounts which incorporate a pad or pads for bonding stones.

Always ensure that a brooch pin is positioned to be above the centre point of your stone—this will avoid the stone tilting forward in an unattractive way. Remember too that looking at the back of the brooch, the pin should always point to the left. Most types are available with a safety catch.

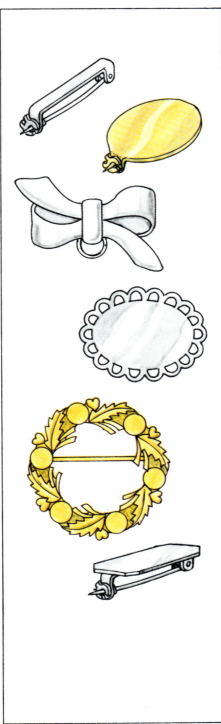

Far Left *17. A plain pendant is intended only to mount and show off a stone. Cast pendants are sometimes ornate enough to wear without a stone.*
Left 18. Common types of brooch mounts: narrow bar for a row of stones, oval flat pad for a large stone, bow-shaped fob brooch for bellcap and stone, brooch with decorative outer border and slightly recessed flat pad is suitable for chippings, wreath-shaped brooch with six flat pads for small tumbled stones.

49

Detailed instructions are given opposite on how to make this beautiful and very personal piece of jewellery.

Part II—Making jewellery from ready made settings and findings

You do not need to be a designer, goldsmith or lapidary to make gem set jewellery. As previously discussed, the range of findings currently available make it a comparatively easy task to assemble pendants, ear-rings, bracelets, rings, key rings and cuff links, incorporating semi-precious stones.

To make the pendant

The assembly of jewellery from findings is best explained by illustrating how to make one particular item, for instance a pendant similar to the one in the picture.

You will need:

A large appropriately shaped polished gemstone.

A bell cap and a jump ring or spring bail.

A neck chain preferably with a bolt ring.

A pack of epoxy resin.

Tools

An abrasive stick or piece of an old grinding wheel.

Some fine nosed pliers or forceps.

A solvent such as methylated spirits, cleaning fluid or lighter fuel.

☐ First decide the way your stone must hang, then press your bell cap over the top part of the stone, gently moulding the cap to the stone. Keep the ring of the cap parallel to the face of the stone.

☐ Abrade the small area of the stone under the bell cap, to give keying for the adhesive, using the abrasive stick or silicon carbide paper. Finally, thoroughly clean the stone and bell cap with solvent to remove finger grease.

☐ Using a match stick, apply the smallest adequate amount of mixed resin to the inside of the bell cap in the predetermined position and gently press the claws against the stone.

☐ When using normal setting epoxy resin, ie one which will require some time to set, a baking tray filled with sand or salt is useful to prop up the stones in an upright position, and the tray may be placed in a cool oven to speed up the curing process.

☐ Faster setting resins, ie that will set in 5–10 minutes, allow the cap to be hand-held until fixed. Also available are several excellent 'instant' adhesives, which will set in about

Right *A selection of rings, using mounts. Instruction on how to make them are given opposite.*
Far Right *Some more ideas on how to use tumbled stones—a pretty bracelet and key ring. Both can be made in the same way as the pendant and rings.*

10–30 seconds.

☐ The above adhesives have advantages and disadvantages but all may be used successfully for jewellery if the manufacturer's instructions are carefully followed.

☐ When the resin is set and any excess removed with tip of a blade, open up a jump ring and place through the bell cap ring. Finally thread the chain through the jump ring and you have created a unique piece of jewellery.

To make the rings
You will need:

A collection of stones, as pictured or to your choice
Ring mounts, to your choice
Epoxy resin adhesive

Tools

As above

☐ Wash the stones in warm water and detergent to remove dirt and grease, then rinse and dry thoroughly.

☐ Mix the resin according to manufacturer's instructions, then apply to both the finding and the part of the stone you wish to face the finding. Wipe off any excess glue.

☐ If you are using a claw mount, bend the claws into position with jewellery pliers or tweezers before inserting the stone. When the stone has been inserted, bend them firmly over it.

The above simple steps may be used for any of the many available jewellery settings, whether using baroque shaped tumbled stones or calibrated cabochons (domed stones of standard shape and size).

A further possibility is to use genuine antique settings for your gems. Occasionally in a junk shop or on a market stall or even in an old box in the loft, one comes across a pretty Victorian setting with a broken or lost stone. Sometimes the 'stone' is glass paste, the foil backing of which has become discoloured, and this too, might be successfully replaced with a modern semiprecious cabochon. (Before breaking up an old piece, however, it might be as well to get it valued by an expert first.) Modern ready made cabochons are calibrated in millimetres, eg 14 × 10 or 20 × 15mm., but it is often possible, with a little judicious grinding on the girdle to make one fit an old setting.

The turquoise brooch illustrated was an antique setting that had lost its stone and the turquoise cabo-

Junk shops or market stalls can provide real finds for enthusiastic jewellery-makers. The setting for this stunning brooch was the result of a particularly successful trip to a local market, and the stone was inserted later.

chon had to be specially cut. With this particular setting a secure mounting was made with a good push fit and no glue was required. The technique to get a good fit is to draw round the inside of the setting on to the slabbed gemstone, using a fine aluminium pencil. If the setting had had a closed back then a pattern could have been produced by placing paper over the setting and rubbing over the centre with a soft pencil or crayon. The pattern could then be cut out in plastic self-adhesive tape and stuck to the slab. The trick is always to cut the stone just a fraction too large for the setting and then to trim the girdle carefully back to give a good fit.

Part III—Wire-Wrapped Jewellery

Another method of making attractive personalized jewellery from rocks and gemstones, is wire-wrapping.

Tumble the stones or pebbles you want to use, as described in Chapter 2, then select the stones you want

Tumbled jasper stones have been carefully matched to make up this necklace. The stones are glued into bellcaps.

to use for a necklace, for example, and arrange them in the sequence that you will link them together. The stones should be fairly similar in size and shape, or else the smaller stones should be towards the ends with the larger ones in the centre. The larger the stones the less you will need but don't make them too large as the weight will be uncomfortable to wear.

To link the stones use wire that will hold them securely, ie the larger the stone, the thicker the wire should be. You can use any wire but try to find some that shows off the stones at their very best. Rough stones do not need very fine wire but smaller, smoother stones will look better in a fine wire, such as silver. You can use brass, copper, silver, silver-plated or even fuse wire.

Basically the method used here to assemble the jewellery is to wrap each stone in a wire 'cage' and then to link them with a series of jump rings. The wire does not have to be perfectly straight but it is easier to handle if it is. To straighten a piece of wire twist one end around a secure object and, using a pair of pliers, pull the other end until it feels as if the wire is stretching. This will remove most of the kinks from the wire.

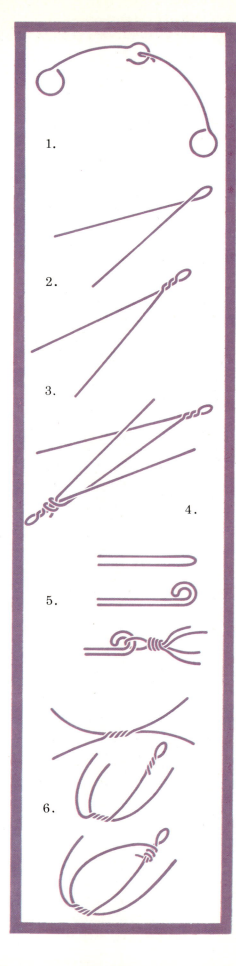

1.

2.

3.

4.

5.

6.

To make the necklace

The method described here for making the necklace can also be used for a bracelet or ear-rings. The ear-rings will need findings from a jeweller to complete the assembly. For an average-sized necklace the complete length should be about 55cm. (22in.).

You will need:

Jump rings, 1cm. (⅜in.) diameter, about 19.

A selection of stones or pebbles.

1.5mm (gauge 15) silver-plated wire.

Tools

Round-nosed pliers.

Side or diagonal wire cutters.

Metal file.

To wrap the stones. You will need about 15cm. (6in.) of wire to wrap around each stone, depending on its size. The wire should be longer rather than shorter as you can always cut off the excess but if it is too short the entire piece of wire will be wasted.

☐ Arrange the stones in the sequence you want to use them, leaving a gap of 2cm. (¾in.) between each one.

☐ Using the round-nosed pliers make a loop at one end of the wire to hold the jump ring.

☐ Hold this to the stone in the position you want it. Bend the length of wire around the stone, working from the looped end and holding it tightly in position. Work towards the other end of the stone, bending the wire to follow the curves of the stone.

☐ Make a loop at the other end and cut off any excess wire.

Make sure that there are no sharp pieces of wire sticking out as they will catch on clothing or scratch the skin.

☐ Make the jump rings (you can use bought ones) and assemble the stones. Depending on the necklace length you require, use one jump ring between each stone, or three for a longer length, but always use an odd number otherwise the stones will not hang as planned. Make sure the front of the stone will face the correct way when assembled.

To make the ends. Measure the length of the arranged stones and subtract this length from the length of the completed necklace. This will give you the length required for the two ends. Say it is 15cm. (6in.), then 7.5cm. (3in.) must be the length of each completed end.

☐ Add 4cm. (1½in.) to the end length and cut the wire. File any sharp ends.

☐ Make a large loop at one end of each piece using the round-nosed pliers. These will be attached to jump rings to assemble the necklace.

☐ At the other end make a U-shaped bend and turn the ends slightly away from the longer length. Shape the entire length so that the two pieces will hook into each other (fig.1).

Bracelet and ear-rings

Very little equipment is needed for this simple bracelet. You can use any tumbled stones you like but choose ones that are roughly the same size and shape, with blending colours.

You will need:

0.8mm (gauge 20–21) silver wire, 1.2m. (4ft.).

5 silver jump rings, 0.6cm. (¼in.) diameter.

If you want to make your own jump rings use 1mm (gauge 18) wire.

Bolt ring clasp and findings for the ear-rings, available from craft stores or jewellers.

About 8 tumbled stones.

Tools

Round-nosed pliers.

Side or diagonal cutters.

The length of the bracelet. Measure the wrist with a tape measure and to this length add 5cm. (2in.) to allow for the bulk of the stones and for comfort. If this measurement is over 19cm. (7½in.) you will probably need six stones, if less, only five. If there is any doubt lay the stones in a row, allowing 2cm. (¾in.) between each one and 0.6cm. (¼in.) to spare at either end. This will give you the final length required.

To wrap the stones. For each stone cut two pieces of silver wire both 10cm. (4in.) long. Bend one piece in the middle (fig.2).

☐ Hold the straight ends in the fingers and the loop with the pliers. Twist round in a full circle to make the loop secure. Repeat with the other pieces of wire (fig.3).

☐ Lay two pieces side by side with the loops at opposite ends and take one straight end and twist it round the base of the loop nearest it (fig.4). Do the same with the other end. Take care that the wire lies flat and

makes a neat twist. Snip off the end after two complete turns and press in the end.

☐ Do the same to the other ends, thus making a wire cage with a loop at either end. The wires of the cage should be pulled out to form an oval shape so that the tumbled stone will slip inside easily, allowing a small space at either end.

☐ Holding the stone inside the cage, grip the wire with the pliers and make a zig-zag shape that lies flat on the stone. This will take a little thought and practice so study the stone carefully so you can show off its shape to advantage.

This bending shortens the wires so that the twisted loops sit snugly at either end of the stone. A gentle half twist of the pliers will tighten them further.

☐ Repeat all this with each of the stones for the bracelet.

To join the stones together open a jump ring just enough to slide the loop of two stones through it, then press together firmly. Repeat with all the others.

☐ Attach the bolt ring clasp to one end to complete the bracelet.

As an alternative to the bolt ring clasp you can make a hook from a piece of wire. Double 4cm. (1½in.) of wire and press the fold as close together as possible. Cut the straight ends even. Using the pliers turn these ends into a loop which goes through the loop at the end of a stone. Bend the loop down to make a hook (fig.5).

The ear-rings are made on the same principle as the bracelet, but the cages are made with a loop at one end only.

☐ Take two pieces of wire 9cm. (3½in.) long and twist them together with three turns in the middle.

☐ Bend all four ends upwards and with one end make a loop with the pliers, twisting the wire back on itself to secure. The end of this loop is laid down the wire and the other ends twisted neatly around it three times and then cut off and pressed down (fig.6).

☐ This makes the cage for the tumbled stone, so proceed to secure the stone as before. This time make sure that the twist at the bottom does not get pulled to one side when the wires are bent into shape.

☐ Connect the loops to the findings to complete the ear-rings.

Other Projects

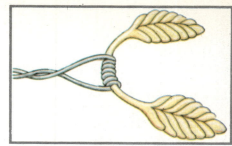

1. *Reel wire 'twig' secures finding.*

Apart from their obvious place in jewellery making, baroque tumbled stones can be used very effectively to make and decorate other things for use in the home and office, and to provide unique and original presents.

Simply gluing the stones on to a flat surface is very easy. Designing your decorations is fun—and it need not be expensive. In fact, it is particularly rewarding to see how a 'throw-away' object can be transformed by a little imagination and a few well-chosen, gleaming stones. Non-returnable packaging, although intended for the waste paper basket, is often well designed and quite sturdily constructed—so you can get long life and much pleasure from re-cycling it.

Re-cycling plastic containers

The plastic containers in which cosmetics are sold are often very prettily shaped, and can easily be turned into highly attractive and personalized jars and pots that warrant pride of place on the dressing table or elsewhere.

Thoroughly clean the jar in warm soapy water, soaking off the manufacturer's labels. Dry well and, if you feel the jar should be a more interesting colour, paint it with a shade chosen from a range of paints sold by model shops for plastic model kits.

Choose stones with one flattish side and glue them on to the surface to be decorated with epoxy resin adhesive, using the same procedures as for jewellery making (see Chapter 5).

It is usually most effective—and cheaper too—to use a few gemstones only. The shapes of cosmetics jars and pots are often so decorative in themselves that just one simple motif or your monogram on the lid, possibly repeated on the side of the jar, is enough. Too many stones and too intricate a design can look overdone.

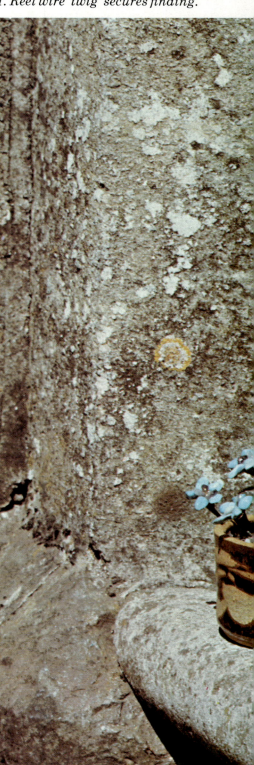

Right *Bonsai tree from gems or 'gemsai'. They come in complete kits or you could design your own tree, using findings, small stones and driftwood—plus wire and plastic adhesive tape from florists and gardening shops.*

2. *Add tape and tiny stones to complete.*

3. *Paper adds bulk to wire branches.*

4. *Detail showing flower shaped finding.*

Right *Boxes can gain a new lease of life with stone and metallic braid decorations. To 'antique' a plastic box, spray with gold paint and then, when it is dry, coat with black boot polish. While still tacky, dust it with a mixture of talc plus green and grey powder paint colours. Next day buff to polish it.*

Below *Plastic pots (flower pots, margarine or yogurt tubs) can be painted and bejewelled to make useful and inexpensive containers.*

Some cigarettes are sold in plastic drums. These can be given the same treatment and, once decorated, revert to their original role or become elegant holders for pencils and pens. Even margarine tubs, yogurt pots and disposable plastic drinking cups can be turned into attractive little vases or (with the bases pierced for drainage) containers for potted plants or growing herbs. The plastic screw-top lids of old glass coffee jars can also be decorated and the jars used as attractive containers for bath salts or coloured cotton wool balls for display in the bathroom.

Wine bottle table lamps
Coloured glass makes a lovely background for showing off polished tumbled stones, and old wine bottles studded with stones can make inexpensive and very attractive table lamps. Many shops sell lamp fittings with adjustable cork or plastic stoppers which can be pushed into the neck of the bottle. If you don't want the flex to dangle down the side, ask a glazier to drill a hole in the side, near the bottom of the bottle, wide enough for the flex to pass through from the inside. Remember to ask him to smooth off the edges of the hole as rough edges are liable to cut into the flex.

For stability the best kind of bottle is a large flagon with a solid broad base. If you do choose a slim, elegant wine bottle either seal the gap between flex and glass and then fill the bottle with sand, or be sure to put the lamp in a place where it cannot easily be knocked over.
If the stones are too big, they will not fit the convex curve of the bottle,

62

can be bought quite cheaply or you may have some about the house—old biscuit tins, sweet tins, tobacco and cigarette tins, wooden date, Turkish delight, glacé fruit or cigar boxes left over from a festive treat. Handsomely decorated, they can make charming presents—really small ones make delightful pill boxes, medium-sized ones provide pretty storage for things such as hair-pins or stamps, and a larger one (lined with a thin layer of foam covered with a remnant of silk or velvet) would make the perfect jewel case in which to keep your own tumbled stone jewellery.

If a wooden box is at all rough, smooth it by sanding, then apply a coat of wood primer. When this is dry, paint the box with clear

so choose smallish stones, with one fairly flat side. File the flattest side of each one (or sand with coarse glasspaper if the stones are soft) and use a contact adhesive such as Bostik 3.

Jewel studded candlesticks

The soft glow of candlelight is also good for emphasizing the rich colours of tumbled stones, and jewel studded candlesticks look very attractive.

Spiked metal candlesticks for large fat candles are available from many chain stores as well as craft shops. Some are shiny and look like brass, and others have a matt black finish. Since they are always small, you won't need many stones even if you decide to cover the metal completely. Don't worry about the thought of spilt wax. This can be washed off the stones quite easily with hot soapy water. But do take care to dry the candlesticks thoroughly, or the metal may corrode.

Buy a candle of suitable width and height for the candlestick. Place it on the spike and draw round it with a pencil. Remove the candle and replace it with a protective cork, then stick your stones in position using an epoxy resin adhesive. Colours can match or contrast with your candle, and the pattern can be anything you like—but be sure to stick all stones outside the pencilled circle only, or your candle will not fit!

Decorating boxes

Plain boxes made of wood or metal

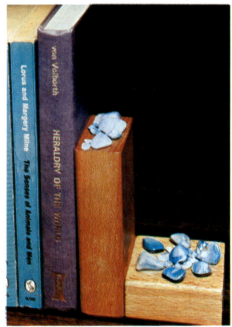

polyurethane varnish if you want to keep the natural appearance of the wood. Alternatively, use gloss, satin or eggshell finish paint in a colour to match or complement the stones you intend to use.

A largish area offers the opportunity to create a 'flower picture' in gemstones. Or you may prefer to make an abstract design, or to scatter tiny chippings of multi-coloured stones to form a mosaic.

Whatever the design you choose, and whether the box is metal or wood, stick the stones with epoxy resin adhesive following the manufacturer's instructions closely.

Making a mirror frame

Mirror and picture frames are other

flat surfaces that lend themselves to decorating with polished tumbled stones. If you already have a plain flat wooden frame you can of course use this but it is not difficult to make your own very attractive and unique mirror. Buy a piece of mirror glass in the size you want from a glazier or a do-it-yourself shop, and a piece of chipboard (not hardboard as it may warp) which is a little larger than the glass and about 1.3cm. ($\frac{1}{2}$in.) thick.

Smooth the edges of the chipboard with medium grade glasspaper. Centre the mirror glass on the front of the board and trace a pencil line round it on the board to indicate where you will finally position it. The outer area, on which you will mount your tumbled stones, will act as a 'frame' for the glass.

Unless you plan to cover the chipboard frame very closely indeed with stones, you will probably want to finish it in some way first to make a more attractive background.

You could paint the chipboard with a coat of gloss or matt paint (having used first a suitable primer). Remember to carry your paint a little beyond your pencilled lines so there is no unsightly gap between mirror and 'frame'. When the paint is dry, stick the mirror glass into position with epoxy resin adhesive and decorate the painted area with stones.

Alternatively you can obtain a richly textured effect by covering the 'frame' with a remnant of velvet or hessian, pulled taut and tacked on to the back of the chipboard. Again there should be an overlap—the fabric must continue just under the mirror glass. The thickness of the fabric overlap will, however, prevent you from being able to

Left *Make paperweights or immerse stones in water—the simplest way to keep tumbled polished stones in gleaming condition. Mix stones for random patterns, graduate in layers according to size and colour, or use one type of stone accordingly.*
Below *Three pours are needed to semi-embed a stone in plastic resin. The first pour must be deep enough for the stone to show above the top of the mould.*

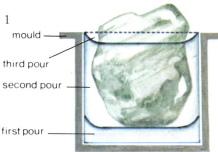

1
mould
third pour
second pour
first pour

stick the mirror glass directly on to the chipboard. So you will have to cut to size a piece of very thin plywood—about 0.2cm. ($\frac{1}{16}$ in.) is about right if velvet is used—and stick this into the rectangle of chipboard. Then stick the mirror glass on to the plywood.

A variety of sizes and shapes of stones can be used to decorate your mirror. They will look best and will

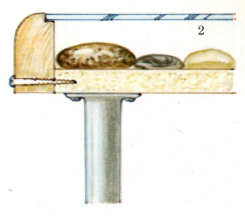

A glass table top is set in a rebate, cut into the wooden frame, well above the top of the largest stone. Stones are set in cement on chipboard and a metal leg is screwed into the chipboard at each corner.

stick more easily if they have one fairly flat side—and you do not need to use many stones to obtain delightful results.

Attach two screw eyes to the back of the board through which picture wire or cord can be threaded for hanging the glass. If ordinary picture cord is used, fix the hangers low enough to completely hide the cord behind the mirror. Or use a pretty cord, such as a macramé cord, in a colour that tones with the stones, and make it long enough to be seen.

Gemstone bonsai trees

Very small tumbled stones can be used to make a glamorous gemstone variation of Japanese bonsai— gnarled dwarf trees—with little leaves or flowers fashioned from polished stones.

Kits, complete with hand-thrown pots, are available by mail order or you can have great fun gathering together the materials yourself.

Use small flattish stones approximately 0.6cm. (¼in.) long to represent leaves or petals, and smaller but not necessarily flat stones in a contrasting colour for buds or flower centres.

Bond the stones on to leaf bails or flower shaped findings with epoxy resin adhesive as in jewellery making, but first secure each finding to a length of soft wire and cover the wire with adhesive tape (preferably in a natural shade of green or brown with a matt finish) to look like a stalk or twig.

To do this, bend a 10cm. (4in.) length of wire in two. Place the loop over a finding and wind the wire over and round until finding is firmly attached (fig.2). Then wrap adhesive tape round the wire stem. Glue the gem studded stems or twigs on to a piece of gnarled driftwood. cleverly placing them so they appear to sprout naturally from it. Alternatively, twist and wrap more wire on to the end of your twigs to make branches and a tree trunk. Before covering the wires with tape, wrap a little soft lavatory paper round them to give thickness. Use scraps of crumpled kitchen foil here and there between the layers of paper to create the gnarled appearance so characteristic of bonsai trees (fig.3). Then cover with gutta-percha tape (floral).

Plant your tree in a pot filled with soil or plastic foam and cover it with green moss for a natural and attractive finish.

Clear cast embedding

Everyone has seen dried flowers, shells, coins and other objects embedded in transparent plastic resin to make things like paperweights and bookends. Tumbled stones can also be treated in this way—and very handsome they look too. However, as tumbled stones are pleasant to touch as well as to look at, you can make a pleasing variation by semi-embedding the stones in the resin, so that the top surface is raised.

To semi-embed a stone in resin, follow the detailed instructions supplied with resin and catalyst kits but remember that the open end of the mould will be the top of your paperweight, from which the best facet of the stone will protrude.

Make the first pour sufficiently deep so that, when placed on it, the stone will show above the top of the mould. Add the second pour in the usual way and leave to dry. The surface will remain slightly tacky and, because resin shrinks, it will be convex shaped and just below the top of the mould. To get a proper finish it is necessary to make a third pour. Mix a small amount of resin with a slightly higher proportion of catalyst than usual. Carefully pour or brush this on to the tacky surface surrounding the stone and leave to dry. It will now cure to a smooth finish (fig.1).

Self-hardening clays

Stones can be set quite easily into self-hardening clays such as Das and Coolclay, which do not need to be fired but harden naturally when exposed to air. These clays can be painted with gouache, poster paints or Indian inks, and manufacturers

can supply special clear varnishes for a glossy finish.

Clay is shaped by hand, of course, so you can choose shapes that you could not make with a mould. A large monogram, for example, would make a highly personalized paperweight. Or you could make an amusing one in the shape of your hand, studding the fingers with stones to look like rings. You could add stones to a dish-shaped piece of clay to make a bejewelled ashtray, or make a doorplate by using chippings to spell out the number or name of your house on a flat clay tablet.

Cementing stones

Stones can also be successfully embedded in cement—to produce anything from a decorative teapot stand to ornamental paving.

Tabletops. In the case of a table top, the problem of producing a flat finish can be overcome in one of two ways.

The table can be designed like a showcase so that the actual table top is a sheet of glass or Perspex.

If this sheet does not touch the stones themselves, but is set into a rebate cut into the frame, it does not matter whether or not the surface of the stones is level (fig.2). Alternatively, the stones can be used to form a decorative border to a slate or tile topped table. A level top surface to the stones is un-important here since the central, major, part of the table offers plenty of flat surface on to which objects can be placed safely.

Bond stones (and tiles or slate) on to a sheet of hardboard or block-board with cement.

Cover the board with an even layer of cement—about 0.3–0.6cm. ($\frac{1}{8}$ to $\frac{1}{4}$in.) thick. Firmly press the stones into the cement and leave till thoroughly dried. Then clean and grout.

You can either make your own table base or buy a metal table frame from a DIY shop. Choose one with holes drilled into the angle irons so that the table top can be screwed neatly and quickly into position.

Naturally tumbled stones. Although a large area decorated with baroque tumbled stones undoubtedly looks very handsome, it can work out rather expensive. But do not let the thought of high costs deter you from tackling a large area. Natural-

Naturally tumbled stones are worth collecting. You can use them as they are, or buff them with wax so that they will shine, then seal them with a coat of varnish. They are particularly useful for decorating large areas, where the use of more precious stones would be very expensive—a table-top or patio for instance. For a patio embed large stones deep into the cement so that the top surface of the stones is fairly level, otherwise you will find your paving uncomfortable to walk on.

Leather thongs and tumbled stones make a very pretty—and unique— covering for this kitchen shelf.

ly tumbled stones are available for nothing from the seaside or river bed. Worn smooth by a fast running river, or pounded against each other by waves on the beach, these stones —although not precious—are often beautifully coloured and interestingly shaped, and make effective decorations.

Varnished, they make a rich looking table top, as can be seen in our

photograph, or leave them in their natural, unglazed state for paving.

Pebble pavements. In parts of Greece almost every village house has a courtyard and, sometimes, interior rooms paved with local stones. The stones are evenly sized to minimize the discomfort of walking on them, usually sugar almond shaped and laid on their sides in a cement bed. Each courtyard has a

different design: the family name, geometric shapes or a symbol, which is 'drawn' in the more unusual black or red coloured stones, against a background of white pebbles. Very simple but very effective—and an idea which is easy to copy.

If you are really ambitious you could cover an entire patio this way, but this form of decoration looks just as good on a small scale. Remove one paving stone and replace it with a pebble mosaic, or surround a tree.

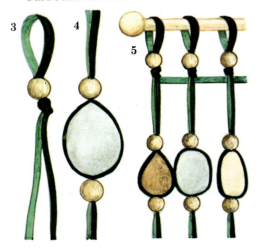

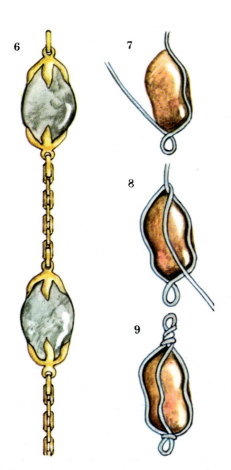

Leather thonging and macramé

Another way in which a collection of stones can prove functional as well as decorative is to use them for bead-type curtains combining the stones with thonging or macramé.

Use polished baroque stones or naturally tumbled pebbles, or both. Pieces of shisha glass (Indian mirror glass) could be used here and there to create a feeling of light and movement.

Make a small curtain to hide untidy shelves. Or, if you live in a small flat where space is at a premium, it might be a nice idea to replace a door with a full-length fringed, bazaar-like curtain. Use as many or as few small stones as you wish. You can use stones at the bottom of your curtain only, or at intervals down it. Always use your largest stone at the bottom of the curtain to give weight, and be careful to avoid heavy stones at eye level where they could cause accidents.

You will need:

A rod for hanging the curtain, and a pair of wall brackets.

A piece of leather thonging cut to the length of the rod.

Leather thonging cut into a number of pieces each twice the length you wish the finished curtain to be plus 15cm. (6in.) or more depending on the length of the curtain.

Stones—as many as you wish.

Wooden beads, twice as many as there are stones, pierced with holes just large enough for two pieces of thonging to pass through them.

Epoxy resin adhesive.

Left *3. Thread a bead on to double thonging, leave a loop for the curtain rod and make a knot below the bead. 4. After an interval, thread a second bead on to the double thonging. Place a stone immediately below the bead. Pull thonging tightly round the stone, using adhesive to stick it, and thread another bead immediately below it for added security. 5. Thread the curtain rod through the loops and stick a piece of thonging parallel to the rod just below the top row of beads. This will ensure that the curtain hangs in an evenly spaced manner.*

Below Right *Tumbled stones are used in conjunction with leather thonging to make this pretty necklace; they are bound together by the same method as the curtains.*

Below Left *6–9. Curtains and jewellery can be made by using bellcaps and chains or—if the stones are too awkwardly shaped to use this method—by wrapping each stone with wire as above.*

Take a piece of thonging and fold it in half lengthways.

Thread both cut ends through one bead and push the bead up the thonging until it leaves a loop at the top large enough to comfortably take the rod from which the curtain will hang. Tie a knot below the bead (fig.3).

Thread a second bead on to both cut ends of thonging and push it up to the point where you want your first stone to be.

Place the stone just below this bead. Spread glue on the inside of both pieces of thonging and draw the thonging tightly either side of the stone.

Thread and push a third bead up the thonging until it rests just below the stone. Pull taut so that the stone is securely sandwiched between the two pieces of thonging and therefore prevented from riding up or falling down the curtain (fig.4).

Continue threading beads and securing stones at intervals of your choice. Then end by threading a single bead on to the bottom of the curtain length and carefully tying a knot.

Polished pebbles placed in jars can make pretty ornaments for desks or window sills. And a large pebble can easily be put to use as a paper weight.

Left *Those pebbles that don't merit tumbling and polishing, can gain a new lease of life and enhance a window sill or shelf or pot. Just arrange them decoratively in or around a dish, and paint a few of particularly good shape into any design that takes your fancy.*
Below *A large stone pebble is halved to reveal its intricate composition.*

When all the other double lengths of thonging have been decorated in the same manner, thread the rod through the loops at the top of each length.

To keep the curtain hanging in an evenly spaced manner, glue the piece of thonging equal to the length of the rod and stitch it just across the curtain, parallel to the rod, just below the top row of beads (fig.5).

Macramé string could be used in place of leather thonging, and, of course, either method could be used for making necklaces, key rings and bracelets.

Wire wrapping stones
Alternatively, suitably shaped stones could have a bellcap bonded on to each end, and then be linked to each other by jump rings and chains (see Chapter 5, Part III, pages 55–59).

Awkwardly shaped stones unsuitable for gluing to bellcaps can be wire wrapped instead, using the following method.

Cut a piece of wire about six times the length of the longest side of the stone.

Leaving about 4cm. (1½in.) of wire at the top, bend the wire around and down one side of the stone and round the stem twice. Cut off any excess.

Make a loop from the stem. Wrap the end round base of loop once and cut off excess (see fig.8 on the previous page).

Index

Pictures supplied by:
Lesley Ansell: 39;
Australian News & Information
    Bureau: 18T;
Steve Bicknell: 28; 30; 31;
British Museum: 7/Peter Clayton;
    9R; 11BR;
Camera Press: 24;
Robert Estall: 23;
Barbara Firth: 65; 66;
Geological Museum/Carlo Bevilacqua:
    21;
Melvin Grey: 64; 67;
Sonia Halliday: 18/19;
Nelson Hargreaves: 29; 34B; 69; 70;
Martin Hayden: 16/17;
Peter Heinz: 59/60; 61; 62;
HMSO: Crown Copyright: 14;
Michael Holford: 5R; 9L;
    11BL/Fitzwilliam Museum,
    Cambridge; 15/Museum für
    Volkerkunde, Munich;
Denis Inkersole: 37; 38/9; 40/1; 54/5;
Institute of Geological Sciences: 4;
    20; 36;
Paul Kemp: 43;
Trevor Lawrence: 58;
Sandra Lusada: 55; 57B;
Bill McLaughlin: 52; 70T;
Dick Miller: 32;
Musee Nacionale de Anthropologia,
    Mexico: 10;
Alisdair Ogilvie: 57T;
Osborne/Marks: 38;
Picturepoint: 22;
Josephine Powell, Rome: 5BL;
courtesy RCF Tools, Birmingham: 27;
F. Salisbury/F. Cotton: 12/13;
Mary Seyd: 68BR;
Spectrum: 18B;
Sunday Times: 8;
Syndication International/
    Womancraft: 50/1; 53; 56;
Paul Williams: 44; 46; 48; 49;

Acknowledgement is given to the
following for articles appearing on
the front cover:
Gill Dutfield;
Gemrocks of Holborn Ltd.;
Natural Gems of London
Endpapers: Natural History
Photographic Agency/Walter
Murray